For Walter Swayze
with Best Wishes
for His Work.

J. G. Nelson

Twayne's English Authors Series

Sylvia E. Bowman, *Editor*

INDIANA UNIVERSITY

Sir William Watson

(TEAS) 45

Sir William Watson

By JAMES G. NELSON

University of Wisconsin

Twayne Publishers, Inc.   ::   New York

For JACK and BOB

Nam in eodem colle ipso alebamur.

Preface

In this, the first full-length study of the life and work of Sir William Watson, I have attempted—in addition to setting forth the important biographical facts—to evaluate his poetry and prose and to indicate his not inconsiderable role in the history of English letters. Since the poet's great years of fame and affluence came during the 1890's, I have devoted the largest portion of the book to a delineation of Watson's rise to fame in 1891 and the qualities of his work and the uniqueness of his literary position which sustained his reputation and significance throughout the last decade of Victoria's reign. After 1900, Watson suffered one of the most incredible declines in the annals of literature and died in 1935 an almost unknown poet. The reasons for his sudden rise to fame and his somewhat spectacular fall, I hope to have clearly and fully set forth; for, in so doing, I think I have indicated something about the momentous revolution in taste which occurred at the close of the Victorian era.

In preparing this study of Sir William Watson, I have had the pleasure of coming to know the poet's devoted wife, Lady Watson, who not only placed at my disposal the Sir William Watson Collection at Yale University, but also gave me the benefit of her knowledge of her husband's life and work. I am indeed grateful to her for the patience, kindness, and good cheer with which she corresponded with me during the progress of this book; and I shall long remember with much pleasure my personal conversations with her at her home, "The Upper Fold," near Asheville, North Carolina.

I also owe my thanks to Sir Shane Leslie of Castle Leslie, Glaslough, Eire, who personally transcribed for me two letters in his possession which Sir William once addressed to Millicent, Duchess of Sutherland. Furthermore, I am indebted to Miss Marjorie G.

Wynne, Research Librarian, The Beinecke Rare Book and Manuscript Library, Yale University, for her kind assistance; and to the Bodleian Library, the Library of Congress, and the Huntington Library, San Marino, California, for permission to quote from various manuscipt materials.

In Madison, I have been aided in my work by several grants from the Research Committee of the Graduate School of the University of Wisconsin, and by the kind and efficient services of Miss Helen F. Northup and Miss Marguerite A. Christensen, both of the University's Memorial Library.

JAMES G. NELSON

University of Wisconsin
Madison, Wisconsin

Contents

Chronology

1858   John William Watson born August 2 in Burley-in-Wharfedale, Yorkshire.

1875   Meets James Ashcroft Noble; visits Tennyson at Farringford.

1876   First published poem, "Poeta Musae," appears in Liverpool *Argus*, October 21.

1880   *Prince's Quest* published in April at father's expense; later in the year poet travels to Continent and North Africa.

1884   *Epigrams of Art, Life, and Nature* published in January.

1885   "Ver Tenebrosum" sonnets re the Soudanese crisis appear in June in *National Review*.

1887   Father dies May 23; Watson turns to criticism for a living.

1888   "The Fall of Fiction," Watson's attack on Rider Haggard's novels, appears in *Fortnightly Review* (September).

1890   *Wordsworth's Grave* appears in Cameo Series in January.

1891   Grant Allen's "Note on a New Poet" in *Fortnightly Review* on August 1 signals Watson's rise to fame.

1892   Engaged to Marian Rolfe Cox, author of *Cinderella*.

1892   Tennyson dies; race for laureateship begins in earnest; Watson one of leading candidates. *Lachrymae Musarum* appears. Gladstone awards Watson £200 grant from Royal Bounty Fund. Mental breakdown occurs at Windsor.

1893   Watson, accompanied by his brother Robinson, goes in January to Switzerland to recuperate from breakdown. In March Elkin Mathews and John Lane publish Watson's *The Eloping Angels* and *Excursions in Criticism*.

1894   *Odes and Other Poems* marks Watson's recovery and return to the front rank of English poets.

1895   Watson moves to London and enters the opulent and busy social and literary life of the city; often resides at John

Lane's rooms at G1 the Albany. In March Lord Roseberry awards Watson a Civil List pension of £100 a year. Watson leads fight in April to force Aubrey Beardsley off the staff of the *Yellow Book;* Lane acquiesces. Fifth volume of the *Yellow Book* (April 30) appears with Watson's "Hymn to the Sea" as the first item; Watson again a leading contender for the laureateship, his influence and power are at their height. *The Father of the Forest* published in November by John Lane. Laureateship battle ends in December with appointment of Alfred Austin.

1896   In *The Purple East* Watson strongly opposes in January government's position on Turkish massacres of the Armenians.

1897   Agnosticism, pessimism in *The Hope of the World* shocks Watson's readers.

1898   Uncle, William Robinson, whom Watson had accompanied to Madeira several years before, dies and leaves the poet a large bequest.

1901   Having recovered from an appendectomy, Watson moves to 13 Caledonia Place, Clifton, Bristol, where he resides until his marriage in 1909.

1902   Watson's celebrated *Ode on the Day of the Coronation of King Edward VII* appears June 13.

1903   Watson's controversial Boer War poems published in *For England* in October.

1904   Watson receives Doctor of Laws degree in April from Aberdeen. The two-volume collected edition, *The Poems of William Watson,* appears in December.

1909   Marries Adeline Maureen Pring on August 11 after a two-week courtship; John Lane is best man. "The Woman with the Serpent's Tongue" appears in October in *New Poems* and various periodicals in England and America. Watson with wife arrives in December in New York; names Margot and Violet Asquith as subjects of "The Woman with the Serpent's Tongue"; later in the month Watson and wife flee to Cuba to avoid repercussions.

1910   *Sable and Purple* published in June.

1912   Watson in New York on February 7 to read poem at Dickens centenary celebration; lectures at Yale and Princeton.

Watson's drama, *The Heralds of the Dawn,* published (May).

1913   First child, Millicent Rhona, born to the Watsons on February 17. *The Muse in Exile* appears in April.

1916   Second child, Geraldine, born to the Watsons on January 29. Watson's prose essay, *Pencraft,* and *Retrogression* are published in November.

1917   Watson's poem on Lloyd-George and other war poetry published in *The Man Who Saw* in May. Watson knighted on June 4.

1919   *The Superhuman Antagonists* appears in September. Watson's volumes on the Irish rebellion, *Ireland Unfreed* and *Ireland Arisen,* published.

1925   *Poems Brief and New* published; Watson's dissatisfaction with England grows; considers moving to America.

1930   Testimonial Fund in poet's honor inaugurated in England on November 3. Watson elected November 13 an honorary corresponding member of the American Academy of Arts and Letters.

1935   Watson dies August 12 at nursing home at Ditchling Common, Sussex. Poet buried August 16 in family tomb in Childwall Churchyard, Liverpool.

CHAPTER 1

Between Two Worlds

> To these succeeds another, newer race,
>   Men light and slight, on narrower scale designed,
> Offspring and image of the change we trace
>   In art, arms, action, manners, morals, mind,—
> The burly oak departing, in its place
>   The lissom willow, swaying to the wind.
>   —William Watson, "After the Titans"

THE last decade of Victoria's reign was in no frivolous or superficial sense *fin de siècle*. It was in the broadest significance of that popular phrase a decadent age, an era of decline; the end not merely of a century but of a great and complex epoch; and the close of an intellectual, social, and artistic tradition. One of the most crucial periods in English history, it was a span of years in which England was visibly failing after having attained unprecedented power, wealth, and prestige during the mid-Victorian years. And despite its brave show of imperialism, its *poètes maudits*, and its "aesthetic shams," an ominous and unmistakable feeling of decline, an aura of melancholy (reminiscent of the begloomed close of Elizabeth's reign) fell across the final years of the nineteenth century. As if by sympathetic magic, the nation's genial spirits drooped; its confidence waned in a burst of feverish reactions as the old queen approached her death.

In these final years when the English nation was literally wandering between a dying world and a new one powerless to be born, a great poetic tradition, too, declined and fell while the first stirrings of the modern poetic idiom were felt. For the death of Alfred, Lord Tennyson in 1892 signaled the end of a great tradition in poetry as surely as the close of the Boer War ten years later marked the end of a great and proud era in British political and economic history. It was during these ten years that the old

Victorian world made its last heroic efforts and finally ceased to be and that the new world of the twentieth century emerged.

Yet the crucial significance of the 1890's has consistently been obscured by the fact that the nervous but showy and superficially confident outward signs of an inward sickness have fascinated later generations. Intrigued and entertained by the decadent flavor of the *Yellow Book*, the "stained-glass" poses of Oscar Wilde, the exoticisms of Aubrey Beardsley, and the cockiness of Kipling, the modern reader has not recognized these posturings for what they often were: the hectic flashes of feverish discontent on the surface of the late Victorian scene.

Behind these ephemeral manifestations and their ultimate cause was the primeval struggle between youth and age, the new and the old. Those who loved and revered the traditions cherished by the Victorians fought a valiant but hopeless battle against those who demanded the right to begin anew and to create a unique, authentic world of their own. In order to focus upon this struggle as it manifested itself in the sphere of poetry and to appreciate the issues involved, one must set aside the popular notion of the 1890's promulgated by numerous nostalgic chroniclers of the era's naughtiness and charm,[1] and view the poetic situation through the eyes of poets and critics who were writing at the time.

Actually there was a surprising unanimity of opinion in the 1890's concerning the development of English poetry and its state. Most critics agreed that there was what they often referred to as a Classical tradition in English literature, within whose bounds the most significant and essentially English poetry had been produced. The chief features of this poetic tradition were generally agreed to be the heroic line with its five heavy accents; a tendency to philosophize and moralize, to maintain a tone of what Matthew Arnold called "high seriousness"; a diction, syntax, and imagery appropriate to this tone; and, finally, a high standard of artistic craftsmanship. Furthermore, the poets in this tradition were often thought of as poet-prophets who, like their Greek ancestors, were "inspired" by the Divine Power of the universe. These writers were, as Gilbert Murray once phrased it, "poets of the higher style" who accepted "the classical, and especially the Greek, tradition as an ideal which they love and to which, however they may adapt and develop it, they endeavour to be faithful." [2] This so-called Classical strain in English poetry was, as Murray indicates, generally thought of as having developed along the lines of the Greek literary tradition rather than the Roman; and, when critics and poets traced the history of English poetry, they often singled out the age of Dryden and Pope as being not only an unfortunate deviation from the main stream of English poetic development but as a period in which the Latin rather than the Greek Classics were emulated.

Often ignoring the earlier development of the heroic line in the works of Chaucer and Spenser, the critics of the 1890's traced the great tradition back to John Milton who was "by common consent," declared Sir Walter Raleigh, "not only a classic poet, but the greatest exemplar of the style in the long bead-roll of English poets." [3] The typical point of view was summed up by Greenough White, when he wrote that

In speaking of a classical tradition in English poetry, which finds its fountain head in Milton, one must premise that he uses the term with a full understanding of its relativity—that he means by it a relatively classic strain in a body of essential romantic poetry. A century after Milton the same fine note, of Hellenic quality that distinguishes it from the Gallic or Latin classicism of Dryden and Pope, was struck again by Thomas Gray, and has never since ceased to sound. This quality may perhaps be best described by the terms restraint and verbal inerrancy—an ethical spirit and a faculty for putting the right word unfailingly in the right place—both derived from contact with the Greek and Latin classics. [4]

The important concept to notice here is that the most perceptive poets and critics from John Keats to Ezra Pound and T. S. Eliot saw that Milton was at the center of this great literary tradition. It was his poetic idiom that pervaded English poetry throughout the eighteenth and nineteenth centuries. In fact, so far as the critics at the close of the century were concerned, the Classical tradition in English poetry could more accurately have been called the Miltonic tradition. We must never forget, cautioned Robert Bridges, "how Milton connects Shakespeare with Keats, how he finally modernized and methodized Chaucer's metrical inventions; how he has been the strongest and most en-

during of all influences on the subsequent progress of English poetry." [5]

Of course, as early as Keats, writers began to feel that this
"most enduring of all influences" was perhaps unendurable; that
such a powerful and pervasive voice in the national poetic tradition was stifling and debilitating. Nevertheless, most Victorian poets had found it possible to display their originality and to add
their bit to the poetic tradition without feeling any baneful effects
of Milton's influence. [6] But after Tennyson and Browning, the last
great poets to work creatively with the heroic line and to con-
tribute significantly to the progress of English poetry, the feeling
that the Classical or Miltonic tradition in English was on the
point of exhaustion pervaded the literary sphere. By 1890 the old
tradition "had become degraded," wrote William Butler Yeats:
"Classical morality—not quite naturalized in Christianized Europe—dominated this tradition at the Renaissance, and passed
from Milton to Wordsworth and to Arnold, always growing more
formal and empty until it became a vulgarity in our time— . . ." [7]

As this startling realization solidified into hard, cold fact, many
poets and critics rising to prominence in the 1890's rejected
what they felt to be a sterile, dying poetic tradition, rebelled
against every feature of the old poetic idiom, and took the first
steps toward establishing a new, suitably modern school of poetry. W. B. Yeats and Ernest Dowson, Thomas Hardy and William Ernest Henley anticipated Pound and Eliot in a desire to
free themselves from the old meters, the time-honored poetic diction, and, in particular, the all-too-pervasive voice of Milton
which threatened to destroy their originality and authentic tone.
The belief was widespread that all that could be done within
the sphere of the traditional school had been done; therefore,
new areas of poetic creativity had to be indicated and explored.

However, the efforts of these rebellious poets to destroy the old
school and to establish a new did not go unchallenged. The 1890's
were still to a large extent ruled by Victorian taste and sentiment,
despite the fact that there were Beardsleys and Wildes. In poetical as well as in critical circles, there was great opposition to
the rebellious elements. By 1890 the principals in the struggle between the "ancients and the moderns" were on the scene, and the
lines were soon drawn. Although the public at large did not be-

come aware of the critical situation in late Victorian poetry until the death of Tennyson in 1892 precipitated the long, controversial laureateship battle, most poets and critics were taking sides and jockeying for position in the ensuing struggle by the beginning of the last Victorian decade.

It was in 1890 that Yeats, Dowson, Arthur Symons, and their fellows formed the Rhymers' Club and began to meet at the Cheshire Cheese to plan their attack upon "everything Victorian." [8] And shortly thereafter in August, 1891, Grant Allen's review of William Watson's first significant volume, *Wordsworth's Grave and Other Poems*, overnight established Watson as the champion of the traditionalist cause. If the Rhymers (often disorganized and disgruntled) were to lead the way toward a modern poetic idiom antithetical to the old, they were to face a formidable challenge from a "True Blue" poet, one William Watson, who, declared Allen, "sails under the good old flag—the flag of Shakspere, Milton, Gray, Burns, Wordsworth. He is all for orthodoxy, patriotism, England, home, and duty." [9]

Among those opposing Watson and the established tradition were many poets whose names were almost unknown at the time but who are now justly famous. Gerard Manley Hopkins, for instance, realized the need for a new poetic idiom based upon contemporary speech patterns. "For it seems to me," he wrote in a letter to Robert Bridges, "that the poetical language of an age shd. [should] be the current language heightened, to any degree heightened and unlike itself, but not (I mean normally: passing freaks and graces are another thing) an obsolete one." [10] Moreover, his development of "sprung rhythm" was a very important and influential step away from the stereotyped use of the heroic line and in the direction of a freer meter more easily adaptable to natural speech. Similarly, Henley, Kipling, Hardy, and Housman reacted against the technical perfection of the old rhythms by experimenting with free verse and the accentual meters which mark their poetry as distinctly modern.

However, the principles of the revolutionaries of the 1890's are most clearly found in the pronouncements of members of the Rhymers' Club. Long before Pound and Eliot enunciated their program for a new poetry, the Rhymers had already set forth upon the path which Pound was later to follow. First, the Rhym-

ers were opposed to what they disdainfully called "rhetoric,"—
the elaborate and ornate "poetic" diction of the traditional idiom.
Second, these poets objected to the habit of "philosophizing"—
that propensity in the poet-prophets to use poetry as a vehicle for
expressing their sentiments and their thoughts on politics, religion, and the state of the universe, generally. Third, the old
rhythms and Latinate syntax were banished, and new meters
coupled with a normal syntax based on the natural language patterns of the day were advocated.

Yeats, the greatest and most important member of the Rhymers' Club, described the revolt against the tradition as one

against irrelevant descriptions of nature, the scientific and moral dis-
cursiveness of *In Memoriam*—"When he should have been broken-
hearted," said Verlaine, "he had many reminiscences"—the political
eloquence of Swinburne, the psychological curiosity of Browning, and
the poetical diction of everybody. Poets said to one another over their
black coffee—a recently imported fashion—"We must purify poetry of
all that is not poetry," and by poetry they meant poetry as it had been
written by Catullus, a great name at that time, by the Jacobean writers,
by Verlaine, by Baudelaire. Poetry was a tradition like religion and
liable to corruption, and it seemed that they could best restore it by
writing lyrics technically perfect, their emotion pitched high, and as
Pater offered instead of moral earnestness life lived as "a pure gem-
like flame" all accepted him for master.[11]

As Yeats indicates, the Rhymers—especially Ernest Dowson, Arthur Symons, and Yeats himself—derived many of their principles of revolt not only from Walter Pater and Dante Rossetti, but
from contemporary French poets such as Verlaine, Rimbaud,
Baudelaire, and Mallarmé. And even though their understanding
of the new *art poétique* came almost entirely through Symons,
they were able to take statements such as Verlaine's *"Prends l'élo-
quence et tords-lui son cou!"* [12] and use it effectively in their re-
lentless attack on "rhetoric," the much despised artificial diction
of the traditional poets.

Likewise, the rebel poets found Mallarmé's dictum close to
their most cherished ideals: "Poetry, my dear Degas, is made not
with ideas, but with words." Poetry must be purified, they in-

sisted, by stripping it down to essentials and by freeing it from
doctrines and detachable thoughts, thus leaving it pure, delicate,
beautiful. Ernest Dowson's verse, devoid of all philosophical or
social preoccupations, with its slightly erotic and bizarre themes,
its delicate verbal tones and nuances, is an interesting example
of the French influence and of how it helped create a poetic
idiom totally antithetical to that of the old tradition. What the
rebels of the 1890's drew from the Symbolists was, according to
Graham Hough, "a preference for slight musical effects, a determination to avoid the poetry of splendid abstractions, Miltonic-
Tennysonian blank verse and the grand style generally." [13]

Although Henley, Kipling, Hardy, and other influential poets of
the 1890's did much to break the hold which the Classical tradition had on English poetry, it was the example and the principles
of the Rhymers which most influenced Ezra Pound who, according to T. S. Eliot, was "more responsible for the XXth century
revolution in poetry than . . . any other individual." [14] Many of
Pound's basic aims, ideas, and tactics were those of the Rhymers
—his attacks on poetic diction, for instance, and his desire to base
the new poetic idiom on the rhythms and language of everyday
speech. The Rhymers were speaking through Pound when he declared, "From the Elizabethans to Swinburne, through all that
vast hiatus, English poetry had been the beer-garden of doc-
trinaires. It had been the 'vehicle' of opinion." And again Pound
was stating principles developed in the 1890's when he declared
the aim of the new poets to be the creation of a "natural speech,
the language as spoken. We desire the words of poetry to follow
the natural order. We would write nothing that we might not say
actually in life—under emotion." [15]

Just how important the Rhymers were to Pound and how much
he appreciated their early efforts is clear from statements in his
letters. "The whole set of 'The Rhymers,'" he once wrote in a letter to Floyd Dell, "did valuable work in knocking bombast, &
rhetoric & victorian syrup out of our verse." Dowson, in particular,
was to him a significant poet in the development of a new poetic:
"To me he [Dowson] holds a very interesting position strategi-
cally, in the development of the art." [16] It was the rebels of the
1890's, then, who actually initiated the momentous revolution in

poetry and laid down the principles and pointed the way to a new poetic style and idiom which, through the efforts of Pound and Eliot, were finally achieved in the twentieth century.

Yeats, looking back on the momentous struggle in the 1890's, was able to say that by 1900 "Victorianism had been defeated." [17] Yet the forces of the traditional poetic idiom—the men who cherished the ideals, the moods, the rhythms, the authentic ring of the Classical school—did not lie down without a fight, nor did they concede defeat when victory was no longer possible. The champion of the forces of the traditional poetic style and idiom, the staunchest, most dedicated warrior in the fight to maintain the prestige and influence of the Classical tradition, was William Watson, the poet who after Tennyson was able to command the largest following and the widest respect among the critics and reading public of the 1890's. Following "Milton and Wordsworth as he would follow a volunteer colonel or an impromptu captain if a foreign army were pouring through the gate of Dover," Watson was convinced, as Gilbert Keith Chesterton once pointed out, "that he [was] standing, and rightly standing, for the whole great historic tradition of English letters and English landscape. He [was] defending it against a host of foreign influences . . . In fighting for the wholesomeness and massive qualities of great English poetry he [felt], rightly, that he [was] fighting for something which [was], like all precious things, in perpetual and incurable peril." [18]

This great tradition was a "precious thing" to Watson because it was literally his life. What nature was to Wordsworth, and the art object was to Keats, the Miltonic tradition was to William Watson, a man who was not really at home among nature, art, or man. There are very few events in his life other than poetic ones which are of much interest and which have much meaning to those of us concerned with Watson's career. We cannot study his life without being impressed by how little else but his work there really was. So it is not surprising to find Watson's love for the tradition and his concern for its future the dominant note in his work. In his "Apologia," he declares, ". . . I have full oft/ In singers' selves found me a theme of song, . . ." His greatest poem, "Wordsworth's Grave," is but one of many in which Watson is concerned with analyzing the work of the great poets of the past and with discovering and pointing out to his readers their distinctive qualities and their essential characteristics. In poems such as "The Sovereign Poet," he exalts the poet-prophet who ". . . sits above the clang and dust of Time,/ With the world's secret trembling on his lip"; and he urges the nation in "England My Mother" to "Slight not the Songsmith" who creates the imperishable songs which inspirit the people.

To save for posterity the authentic tone, the meters which had become a part of the very rhythm of English life, the diction which was to the great majority of Englishmen synonymous with the word "poetry," became Watson's one goal in life. ". . . it is his function," said William Archer, "and his glory to hand on, in this generation, the classical tradition of English poetry." [19]

Consequently, Watson studied and emulated the great classic figures of English poesy, conformed to their pattern, restated their views, caught their tone and rhythms, and sought in every way he could to sustain their music and to pass on their thoughts and attitudes to a generation which he felt needed to keep before it the high standard, the value and worth of this noble heritage. Not by innovation, but by treading "in nobler footprints than mine own," and traveling "by the light of purer eyes," he strove to extend the life and influence of the tradition. Simply by echoing the distinctive notes of the traditional poetic idiom and by creating anew the authentic ring, Watson hoped to stem the tide of time: ". . . if I be indeed/ Their true descendant," he confidently reasoned,

> . . . their lineaments
> Will out, the signature of ancestry
> Leap unobscured, and somewhat of themselves
> In me, their lowly scion, live once more.

In a time of great change and lawlessness, when few were certain of a poetic standard, Watson upheld the traditional poetic idiom as an ideal of enduring and unsurpassable excellence. "We gain from him [Watson]," wrote a contemporary critic, "a welcome reassurance that the great names which in the growing bulk of minor literature have begun to exist for us as names alone, are really the most abiding. He has scant courtesy for the fads and fashions of a shifty generation. Shakespeare, Milton, Wordsworth, our fathers' gods shall be our gods in the tranquil ingathering of the fruit." [20] And in a letter written to Watson in 1894, Churton Collins, a much admired critic, declared, "God be thanked we have at least got you to keep up the good tradition." [21]

Against the innovators' experiments and eccentricities in verse, Watson opposed his classically molded poetry with its epigrammatic phrasing, its latinized diction, its clarity of style and dignity of movement. In his verse and prose, Watson took arms against the "eccentrics," and met "the disdain of the decadents with a disdain equal to their own." [22] In the early 1890's Watson optimistically believed that the readers of poetry were "growing weary . . . of the vaunted exotic graces—and uglinesses—which have been imported with so much pomp and circumstances into English verse." Emphatically he declared: "We do not require these foreign reinforcements: the countrymen of Shakespeare have no need to borrow either their ethics or their aesthetics from the countrymen of Baudelaire; and if we be wise we shall turn more and more to whatsoever singer scents his pages, not with livid and noxious *Fleurs du Mal,* but with the blossoms which English children gather in their aprons, and with the candid breath of our hardy and hearty English sky." [23]

Thus through the 1890's Watson filled the place of Tennyson and Arnold in the hearts of Englishmen who gained solace and assurance from poetry which echoed wistfully the great vibrant poets of their youth. Watson better than any other poet of the time spoke for those who stoically and with faint and clouded hope marched on into the new century with very few of the trappings which once formed a part of their safe and solid mid-Victorian existence.

Free from the bizarre instability of a Wilde or a Beardsley, without the optimistic hardihood of a Henley or a Kipling, unable to attain the religious fervor of a Lionel Johnson or a Francis Thompson, Watson stood virtually alone as the Tennyson and Arnold of the 1890's. To maintain such a position was in an age of eccentricity, as Chesterton once remarked, the only way to be truly original; that is, "not to be original at all." [24] Certainly Watson's conventionality and traditionalism has in time led us to believe that he was something of an anachronism in the 1890's. Yet, viewed from the standpoint of the late Victorian age, it was

Beardsley, Wilde, and the innovators in poetry who were odd. The vast majority of the English were still "Victorians" who tolerated the Wildes up to a point—the corner in which they could crush them.

Watson, often referred to as "the least 'Ninetyish'" of popular poets of the time[25] was, nevertheless, a characteristic product of the period. He was one of those numerous men and women of the *fin de siècle* who "Fated among Time's fallen leaves to stray" found themselves breathing

> . . . an air that savours of the tomb,
> Heavy with dissolution and decay;
> Waiting till some new world-emotion rise, . . .

Despite his early optimism, like so many who have given their all to a lost cause, Watson soon realized that the time-spirit was against him: that he, unfortunately, was at the end rather than at the beginning of the great tradition he so passionately loved. Wistfully the last of an illustrious line turned to the first and saluted him: "For thou art of the morning and the May,/ I of the Autumn and the eventide."

CHAPTER 2

"The Three Voices"

The first voice, then the second, in their turns
Had sung me captive. This voice sang me free.
—William Watson, "To Edward Dowden"

IN OCTOBER of 1770, Thomas Gray, traveling in Yorkshire, came along a high hill and descended into what was then known as the Vale of the Wharf which he described as "well-wooded, well-cultivated, well-inhabited, but with high crags at distance, that border the green country on either hand." In the midst of this rural scene with its winding river, the poet found "a neat and pretty village among trees," Burley-in-Wharfedale, where, nearly a century later, John William Watson was born on August 2, 1858.[1]

His father, who traced his ancestry back to Yorkshire squires of Elizabeth's reign, was, as his son was later to describe him, "a pure practical business man." [2] His mother, who came "of an old stock of Wensleydale yeomanry," [3] was a timid, simple woman whose dreamy, emotional nature contrasted strongly with her husband's. Moreover, Dorothy Robinson Watson was a devout Methodist who loved to memorize long portions of the Bible and to savor its phraseology, style, and rhythm;[4] but her husband John was a confirmed agnostic who read the latest scientific literature with great interest and imparted his enthusiasm to his family.[5] A robust, active extrovert, John Watson was a prosperous merchant and twine-maker in Burley at the time of his son's birth. Two years later, in 1860, he moved his family to Liverpool where he enlarged his interests in the flourishing textile trade.[6] It was here in this fast-growing, ugly, middle-class port city that William, the future poet, grew to manhood amidst surroundings he could hardly have enjoyed.

I *The Early Years*

Unlike his father, Watson was a shy, moody introvert who, because of ill-health, was unable to attend school until he was twelve. Yet, despite his lack of formal schooling, William early showed an unusual susceptibility to literary and musical influences and impressions. His imaginative and artistic nature, which he derived from his mother's side of the family, revealed itself in his skill at the piano and in his delight in reading. When he was six, he read Bunyan's *Pilgrim's Progress;* and by the age of seven, he was writing poetry and composing music;[7] and his extraordinary memory enabled him to memorize Milton's *Paradise Lost* during his ninth year.

His study of these two great staples of mid-Victorian reading, together with his mother's devotion to the Bible, assure us that William Watson was, like so many of his contemporaries, raised in an atmosphere of devout nineteenth-century evangelicalism which evidently, without undue tension, shared the roof with its arch-enemy, agnosticism. While he was learning verses from the Bible at his mother's knee, he was being "cradled in ideas of evolution." Watson was later to recall that he "grew up in an atmosphere where 'natural selection' and 'the survival of the fittest' were household words. My earliest companion in country walks—my father—was a man whose very enfranchised mind had a natural impulse towards scientific speculation on its largest lines, and he did not long leave me unimbued with his own tendencies." [8]

As a consequence of this strange mingling of the mother's Puritanism and the father's agnosticism, the son, unfortunately, was never to have the "enfranchised mind" of the father. Nor was Watson to share any of the important characteristics of this parent. His sensitive, highly emotional nature was to find a congenial atmosphere only among books, music, and nature. Instead of entering the active work-a-day world at the usual age as his brothers James and Robinson were to do, William devoted himself to writing poetry and to developing his musical skills at the piano.

By the age of sixteen, he had turned his back forever on the business world of "getting and spending" and had set himself rigorously to bring his artistic powers to full fruition. Just how dedicated to poetry he was is indicated in a letter written by a Mr. Charles Berry who knew the poet at this time: "In those days, now twenty years ago, Mr. Watson, then a mere youth, was severely discipling himself for the vocation to which he felt himself called. His life from that day to this has been one of uncompromising self-repression, strenuous study, and heroic devotion to the prophetic faculty within him." [9]

Without his father's consent, Watson, naturally, could not have followed such a course. But, like John Milton, the young William was blessed with an indulgent father, who, despite the practical bent of his nature, allowed his son the leisure necessary to follow the call of the muses. Hall Caine, who knew Watson in Liverpool, once wrote that the poet's "father, partly out of regard for his [son's] health, and partly . . . on the recommendation of Edward Dowden, of Dublin University, had left him free to follow, if he wished to do so, the profession of literature." [10]

It was during this first important year of his life, 1875, that the now dedicated young sixteen-year-old set out on the road to Farringford (the path he longed to travel in life) and made his pilgrimage to the court of the reigning monarch of English poetry and the heir of Milton and Wordsworth—Alfred, Lord Tennyson. Ushered into the sanctum by the poet's son, Hallam, the anxious young admirer found the mage composing his drama, Queen Mary, and gazing soulfully out upon the beautiful gardens which surrounded the estate.

During the course of the interview, when Tennyson urged his disciple to write for pleasure but to choose another more materially rewarding vocation, the Poet Laureate could hardly have foreseen that at his death, this frail, ascetic boy would be one of the leading contenders for his crown of laurel. And despite the cautious encouragement, Watson was never to forget this fateful meeting, for the great poet played consummately his role of chief oracle to the nation and treated his humble guest with great kindness and attention.[11]

During this same year in which he visited Tennyson, Watson also came to know James Ashcroft Noble, an essayist and critic of some note who resided in Liverpool. Watson's father, who apparently had some acquaintance with Noble, told the writer about his son's interest in poetry; and soon after Noble invited the aspiring poet to spend an evening at his home and to read his poetry. This Watson did, and Noble was impressed: ". . . there was something both in the personality and in the work of the youthful singer," he wrote some years later, "which so impressed me that I was reckless, or prescient, enough to encourage him to persevere. I saw in the poems he then submitted to me, not merely fluency and fancy, which are common enough in adolescent work, but a certain intellectual grip, which seemed to promise indefinite possibilities of progress—a promise which certain new poems sent to me from time to time amply fulfilled." [12]

Despite Liverpool's dominant tone of commercialism, the city was not wholly bereft of artistic and literary life. Hall Caine, later to become a famous novelist and a friend of Dante Rossetti (but then a young, struggling architect working in the seaport city), founded a literary club known as the Notes and Queries Society which brought together the men and women of Liverpool who were interested in literature. Noble, of course, was a member and soon introduced his young friend, William Watson, to the society. At this time, Watson was anything but the handsome, virile-looking man which he was to become in the 1890's. He was, as Hall Caine recalled, a "very slight and pale, very modest and reticent" youth who constantly reminded those of the literary circle of John Keats, "not alone by his spiritual gifts, but also his physical infirmities, for he was very delicate then, and we feared he would die of decline." [13]

This young Keats, who found the intellectual climate of Caine's literary society congenial, derived much encouragement from its members, especially from Ashcroft Noble who became his first mentor and literary adviser. Noble's home in Liverpool (if it were anything like his later home in London) was "comfortable and pleasant and very cosy, with people always coming and going." His daughter, Helen, once described the family life as "very happy, very social, very united. We were unconventional, though in no startling way—just informal and unselfconscious." [14] This genial, cultivated atmosphere must have been a pleasant refuge for Watson, a bright spot in the midst of the harsher realities of his Liverpool existence. Often the poet spent his evenings in the Noble drawing room either reciting his poetry or playing on the piano the music of Beethoven, Schumann, and Chopin.

Just as his taste in music was "Romantic," so was Watson's taste in literature at this time. His early extant poetry shows that he was reading and imitating a whole host of poets such as Shelley, Keats, Coleridge, Wordsworth, the early Tennyson, Rossetti, Edward Dowden, John Todhunter, and perhaps Poe. Of these poets, Shelley and Keats were his first favorites; and in his poem "To Edward Dowden" Watson later spoke of his early devotion to them:

> In my young days of fervid poesy
> He [Shelley] drew me to him with his strange far light,—
> He held me in a world all clouds and gleams
> And vasty phantoms, where ev'n Man himself
> Moved like a phantom 'mid the clouds and gleams.
> Anon the Earth recalled me, and a voice [Keats's]
> Murmuring of dethroned divinities
> And dead times deathless upon sculptured urn—
> And Philomela's long-descended pain
> Flooding the night—and maidens of romance
> To whom asleep St. Agnes' love-dreams come—
> Awhile constrained me to a sweet duresse
> And thraldom, lapping me in high content,
> Soft as the bondage of white amorous arms.[15]

Certainly the "strange far light" of Shelley and his fervent belief in the powers of poesy mightily appealed to the young, introspective Romantic whose shy, sensitive nature early led him to a painful awareness of the great gulf which separates the real from the ideal. His early poetry often reveals him to be a melancholy, uneasy, rather world-weary young man who prefers a dream world, "a world all clouds and gleams," to the real world "where ev'n Man himself" moves "like a phantom." Furthermore, his early work indicates a predilection for languorous, musical, alliterative, overly poetic verse which creates a wistful, pensive mood and which tends to lull one into a dreamy, visionary state.

II *Early Poems*

Watson's first published poem, "Poeta Musae," appeared on October 21, 1876, in the first number of the Liverpool *Argus*, a rather short-lived journal edited by James Ashcroft Noble and supported by the more intellectually and artistically inclined members of Liverpool society.[16] The poem is an excellent example of Watson's early Romantic vein and was signed John Wilson Maitlaw, an anagram version of his name. It is, appropriately enough, Shelleyan in theme and tone, and the young poet's pose of the world-weary idealist traveling "the long life-path alone" is also reminiscent of Shelley. The poem, which was never again published, is the earliest statement of the poet's life-long devotion to poetry. Certainly it is appropriate that his first published work should have been a kind of dedication to poetry, a celebration of poetry's ability to soothe and comfort and shine "the mist and the midnight away."

> Cheer me and comfort me,
> Spirit of Poesy,
> Aye when I tread the long life-path alone.
> Fold up thy wandering wing!
> Sing, to my spirit sing!
> Sighing and murmuring
> Every wild tone,
> Gladness and sorrow and laughter and moan.
>
> Lap me in melody,
> Spirit of Poesy;
> Lull me with joy-notes and dirges of dole:
> Anthem or madrigal,
> So it be musical—
> Music whose echo shall
> Murmur and roll,
> Murmur and linger and dwell in my soul.
>
> Drowsily, dreamily,
> Spirit of Poesy,
> Whisper when evening descends like a dove:
> When the lorn nightingale
> Sighs out her doleful tale,

With her melodious wail
Telling the grove
All the mellifluous sorrows of love.

Sing to me lullaby,
Spirit of Poesy,
When the deep sea of sleep over me laves—
When my soul floats away,
Floats mid its ocean-spray,
Drifts till the dawning day
Lights up its caves,
Drifts on the foam of its undulant waves.

Ever my solace be,
Spirit of Poesy!
Blend with my soul-dreams by night and by day!
Star of my morn be thou!
Star of my twilight glow!
Shining as fair as now
Ever and aye,
Shining the mist and the midnight away.[17]

Except for the verse form which is original with Watson, the musical movement of the lines, the alliteration, the trite diction and images are similar to the poet's second published work, "Time and Tide," which appeared in the *Argus* three weeks after "Poeta Musae." [18] Like its predecessor, this poem is from the Romantic side of Watson's personality and again presents a picture of a dreamy, aloof poet at home only in the mystical half-light of a visionary world. Perhaps it shows an attraction on the part of Watson for another poet of "glimmer and gloom" and "moonlitten" landscapes, Edgar Allan Poe.

In glimmer and gloom of a moonlitten shore
We walked while the world was asleep,
And we spoke of the passion and pulse of the waves,
And the silence and song of the deep,
And the mystical speech of yon legion of stars,
With the secrets of time in their keep.

And we talked of the poets whose songs have upreared
All beautiful shapes out of dream,

down rules for rhymes.)
w I think of it,
epics, have you writ,
absence?—By the bye,
matters, I
g Prince's Quest—(it weighs
cluding leather-case)—
intent to add thereto,
ncashire and you.
ot done a line; for though
n extra flow
nuine inspiration, somehow
ithin me has lain dumb. (How
continue, there's no judging,
s given no signs of budging,
m getting rather tired
ery day to be 'inspired.')
ust stop. For as I write
he sky is waxing bright
e afternoon has grieved in rain:
h circumstances I am fain
is barren task of spinning rhyme
the meadow-airs till suppertime,
hours that know not any hot sun.
ll for the present.—William Watson.[28]

letter was written, Watson's inspiration did re-
able to finish "The Prince's Quest" during his
. The little-known poet, who naturally enough
ole to sell his manuscript to a publisher, persuaded
ovide funds for the publication of the long poem
orter ones. Despite his opposition to his son's po-
John Watson took his son to London and made
with Messrs. Kegan and Paul to publish the manu-
ue course, therefore, Watson's first volume, *The*
st and Other Poems appeared in April of 1880 bound
h boards lettered in gold and decorated in black. It
some little volume in which "The Prince's Quest" ap-
t and was followed by a shorter narrative poem,
ine lyrics, and four sonnets. "The Prince's Quest," the

"The Three Voices"

> And of those who have sung of the magical sea
> Envestured in glory and gleam;
> Of the sea in its languor of passionless calm
> Or in rapture of tempest supreme.

The Romantic themes, moods, and mental states represented in these early poems were later to contrast sharply with the more Classical, objectively oriented *engagé* poetry which Watson was to write after his sudden, rather startling revulsion from the introspective life of the isolated artist after 1880.

In the same year in which his first two poems appeared, 1876, the Watson family moved to Southport, a town on the Irish Sea about twenty-five miles north of Liverpool. Here Watson, now eighteen, began a three-year term of schooling under the direction of a Reverend Mr. Hall, "who kept a day school in Gloucester Road, Birkdale." The reminiscences of a schoolmate afford us a rare close-up of the poet during these rather obscure years. Watson, who evidently never had any interest in outdoor sports, gave all his attention to books at the school where his major concern "was almost exc[l]usively with his own quick mind, which astonished his companions by its skill in dialectic and the fertility of its ideas." Watson, who solved all the scholar's problems with the greatest of ease, appeared to his fellows to do his "homework" during his short walks to and from school. The fierce pride and somewhat haughty bearing of the later poet were clearly beginning to show themselves at this time and were attributed to his "uncommon self-retentiveness." Although he was "aware of his unusual gifts," his fellows were of the opinion that Watson held them "in great control." [19]

Although Watson was now living at some distance from his literary friends in Liverpool, his contact with them did not cease; and he continued to see much of James Ashcroft Noble who urged him on to greater things. Since both men were now very much taken with the Pre-Raphaelite poets, especially with Dante Gabriel Rossetti and William Morris,[20] it is not surprising to find Watson imitating Rossetti in an unpublished sonnet, "The Triple Lordship," which is very much after the manner of *The House of Life* sonnets. Despite its commonplace phraseology and its obscurity, the theme—the preoccupation with Life, Death, and Love—is Rossetti's.

Three spirits rule this earth and all hereon.
The first is Life, the last is doomful Death;

. . . .

But midway twixt these twain the second stands,
And evermore he sings clear songs, and plays
Upon the lute he holdeth in his hands:
Low voice and sweet he hath as any dove;
And who would learn his name needs only gaze
Up at his eyes, wherein is written *Love*.[21]

As August 2, 1879, approached, the date on which he legally would come of age, Watson must have longed for some wider recognition of his talents than fame had heretofore afforded him. Although two of the Spenserian stanzas from his poem, "Ode on the Fiftieth Anniversary of the Death of Beethoven," had appeared in the London *Graphic* in 1877,[22] he was still an unknown poet. And despite his shyness and introspective tendencies, Watson had ambition which manifested itself as a burning desire to gain a position of importance and consequence in the world. It was, he no doubt felt, the time to come of age poetically as well as legally and to make a bid for national recognition. Meager though his published work was, it was enough—combined with Noble's encouragement and Watson's thirst for recognition—to lure him out upon that enigmatic yet tempting "thorny path of fame." Consequently, he gathered his strength, buoyed up his hope, and fired his courage for the great attempt to gain a place in the world of English poetry.

III *"The Prince's Quest"*

First Watson surveyed the field of contemporary poetry and came finally to look with a good deal of interest on the vogue William Morris had established with his long, pseudo-medieval narrative poems. Although Watson had never attempted anything of length, he and Noble no doubt felt that a long poem which took advantage of the current fashion would be a good risk. Besides, the lengthy narrative would give Watson ample opportunity to display his poetic talents to the full and, at the same time, allow him to indulge his taste for Romantic scenes and moods set in ages and climes remote from the mid-Victorian world of ugly cities and philistine money-makers. Since the venture meant every-

poem on which Watson's hopes rested, is a long narrative poem of 1814 lines, chiefly in loose couplets divided into ten parts with three lyrics interspersed.

The poem, like the poems of his apprenticeship, is a highly derivative work showing the influences of Shelley and Keats, Wordsworth and Coleridge, Tennyson, Milton, and, in particular, Morris. It, like so many of Watson's works, is fairly bristling with echoes, motifs, and the diction of the poets he loved. In fact, the poem is so highly of a derivative nature that it has been difficult for its critics to agree on any one main influence. One says Shelley; another, Keats; and some, Morris. An early reviewer for the *Academy* sought to solve the dilemma by saying that "The Prince's Quest" is told "in pleasant enough Chaucerio-Keatsio-Morrisian verse." [25] Certainly the "Morrisian verse" is here. Watson's loose handling of the heroic line is close to Morris' use in *The Earthly Paradise*. The pseudo-medieval character of the poem—the quest motif, the mage, the enchanted palaces, the magic jewels, the idealistic Prince himself—is modelled after Morris' then famous and widely read romances. Furthermore, the diction, the tone, and the movement of the verse seem to me to be highly reminiscent of Morris' technique.

The poem commences, as one might expect, with a description of a golden world of long ago, a kind of earthly paradise which existed before the world "fell to waxing gray with weight of years/ And knowledge, bitter knowledge, bought with tears,—" The opening lines, beginning with the Wordsworthian echo, "There was a time," describe a dreamy world of innocence

> When it did seem as if the feet of time
> Moved to the music of a golden rhyme,
> And never one false thread might woven be
> Athwart that web of worldwide melody. (II, 131)

The center of the reader's attention, the Prince, who has grown to manhood in this lovely land, is of a nature and sensibility more rare and ethereal than the Hesperian-garden world of his birth. Like Shelley's poet in *Alastor,* he is the typical romantic youth living in, yet not quite a part of, his world. Handsome, yet delicate,

There lurked at whiles a something shadowy
Deep down within the fairness of his face;
As 'twere a hint of some not-earthly grace,
That made this mortal stripling rather seem
The very dreaming offspring of a dream
Than human child of human ancestry:
So hid in moods fantastical was he
Full often! (II, 132)

Like Tennyson's Prince in *The Princess* who often could not distinguish the "shadow from the substance" and "on a sudden in the midst of men and day" found himself moving "among a world of ghosts," Watson's ascetic youth, too, moves about "likest one" who seems "half-sunk in trance,/ That wanders groping in a shadowy land,/ Hearing strange things that none can understand" (II, 140).

For every handsome prince, there must be a princess; and, having seen her in a strange dream-vision, the hero is forever after in love with her. After some dreamy procrastination, he sets out in search of this lady, who—like the object of the poet's love in *Alastor*—is the embodiment of "all of wonderful or wise or beautiful, which the poet, the philosopher or the lover could depicture." [26] Like that of Keats's Endymion and many another idealistic youth's, his quest for his ideal is a long, often painful, frustrating one which takes him into many strange lands and across many a wild, tempestuous sea before he achieves union with his lady.

There has been some question as to Watson's intentions in his first and only long narrative poem. For instance, Richard Holt Hutton, perhaps thinking of the poem in terms of Shelley's *Alastor* or of Keats's *Endymion*, interpreted it as a kind of allegory, a tale which concerns the "ultimate triumph of the inward vision over the outward hindrances." [27] However, Watson, himself, specifically repudiated this opinion. In a conversation with Churton Collins, he once said that he was "too much under the spell of mere sensuousness to invest it ["The Prince's Quest"] with such an allegory as Hutton found in it; . . ." [28]

Despite this apparent difference of opinion, it seems to me that both Watson and Hutton were correct. Although Watson's primary purpose in writing "The Prince's Quest" was, of course, to produce a mature, finished poem which would establish his claim to fame, he no doubt enjoyed an opportunity to indulge his gift for writing sensuous, mellifluous verse and to exercise his "fancy" by drawing out of his marvelous memory almost at will the various harmonies, voices, archaisms, images, and themes of the poets from Milton to Morris whom he loved.

Besides this primary motive, Watson had no other intention than to write a long, dreamy narrative with no purpose but to soothe and entertain his readers and himself, to lull them away with him from a dull, drab, painfully real world of the present to a golden world of the past where wonders occur often and youth and love are eternal. There is no evidence of a moral theme in "The Prince's Quest"; and there is no indication, such as one finds in *Alastor*, or *Endymion*, or "The Lady of Shalott," that the Romantic idealist is wrong when he turns totally away from humanity to indulge his sensitive soul in an ideal world. Thus, Watson was not only close to Morris in the way he handled the heroic line and shaped the movement of his verse; he was in his intention, also, as close as Morris ever came to a real art for art's sake position. After all, what better description of the young Watson and his intentions in "The Prince's Quest" can be found than Morris' own lines prefaced to *The Earthly Paradise*:

> Dreamer of dreams, born out of my due time,
> Why should I strive to set the crooked straight?
> Let it suffice me that my murmuring rime,
> Beats with light wing against the ivory gate,
> Telling a tale not too importunate
> To those who in the sleepy region stay,
> Lulled by the singer of an empty day.

Watson, then, was right when he said that his poem was the result of an effort to write a merely "sensuous" poetry devoid of any moral or esoteric meaning. But whether he was conscious of it or not, his Prince did represent the subjective, world-shy element in his soul—the romantic Watson of "Time and Tide" and of "World-Strangeness." Watson in these years prior to 1880 was certainly at one with the Prince who walked through a world which seemed "remote and unfamiliar," an alien world in which he, himself, seemed "a something from afar,/ Looking at men as shadows on the wall/ And even the veriest shadow among them all" (II,

164). When his idealistic young Prince refuses the responsibilities of his father's realm and goes in search of a timeless world where beauty and love never fade, Watson was, unconsciously painting a portrait of himself as a young artist.

The enthusiasm of Watson and Noble for Dante Rossetti's poetry naturally led the poet to send a copy of his first volume to the famous man who was living at Tudor House in Chelsea. Watts-Dunton, the companion of Swinburne, once recalled that he saw a copy lying on a table in Rossetti's house and urged the poet to read it. According to his brother William, Rossetti was "immensely taken with it, read passages aloud to me, and predicted great things of the young poet." [29] There is no doubt but what Rossetti was very much impressed by *The Prince's Quest and Other Poems*, for he not only despatched a letter of acknowledgment to Watson, but also wrote to Hall Caine saying that the young poet "must not be discouraged . . . with his real and high gifts." [30] Moreover, after Rossetti's death, his annotated copy of the title poem came into the hands of William Sharp who called attention to Rossetti's "markings and marginalia" and to his special liking for the passage in Part Six in which the mysterious "palace builded of black marble" is described. [31]

The reviews of *The Prince's Quest and Other Poems* were disappointingly few, and none shared Rossetti's enthusiasm. The reviewer for the *Academy*, for instance, found the volume to be run-of-the-mill poetic fare. The verse, which he felt was of a kind all too common at the time, was "tinged with the prevailing affectation of archaic language." [32] The reviewer for the *Athenaeum* also found "The Prince's Quest" to be "somewhat disfigured by affectations of diction," but he went on to say that Watson "has, on the whole, done good work." In addition to declaring that Morris' *The Earthly Paradise* was the chief influence on "The Prince's Quest", he pointed out that Watson was "most original and altogether at his best in those portions of his poem which give greatest scope to imagination." [33]

Among the "other poems" in *The Prince's Quest* volume is "Angelo," another narrative tale with a medieval setting. Consisting of 315 lines of pedestrian blank verse, it tells a somber, unhappy tale of an old but kindly nobleman destroyed by the hatred and falseness of his fair, young wife. Of more interest are three

poems which—like Keats's "Ode to a Nightingale" and many another Romantic poem—dramatize the poet's return from a moment of transcendent vision to the harsh world of reality. In "Vanishings," a sonnet, the octave is a simile in which the poet is like
one who having looked upon a splendid, fiery world transformed
by the setting sun suddenly turns eastward and "Sees a lacklustre world all chill and gray." In the sestet, his dream world vanishes, and he beholds ". . . the dreamless world anew:/ Sad
were the fields, and dim with splendours gone/ The strait sky-
glimpses fugitive and few" (II, 208).

The lyric, "A Sunset," is similar to the octave of "Vanishings" in
that a city is dreaming in the glorious fire of a gorgeous sunset.
But the city, too, like the idealist poet, awakes, "Her mighty Fire-
Dream o'er," and looks about "amazed, immobile, dumb." The
poet again dreaming in the sonnet "Skyfaring" is caught up by the
charioteer, Imagination, into his "glistering car." Then

> From shade to shade the wingèd steeds did leap,
> And clomb the midnight like a mountain-sleep;
> Till that vague world where men and women are,
> Ev'n as a rushlight down the gulfs afar,
> Paled and went out, upswallowed of the deep.

But like Keats in "Sleep and Poetry," Watson is unable to sustain
the vision and to follow the "ethereal charioteer" for long:
". . . wakened by ten thousand echoes," he suddenly finds "That
far-off planet [earth] lying all-too near."

Watson's early attitude toward God is revealed in two poems in
the volume, "The Questioner" and "God-Seeking," which reflect a
rather typical Victorian state of mind—the conflict between Puritanism and agnosticism. Despite his father's unbelief, the poet as
a child was thoroughly indoctrinated with mid-Victorian religious
notions. That his brother Robinson became a well-known, popular evangelist is proof enough of the mother's sturdy religious
influence. Consequently, as Watson grew older, his will and desire to believe in God, thwarted by the rational evidence of the
mind, led him, like so many of his contemporaries, into a frustrating state of doubt, questioning, and indecision which was
never completely relieved.

That the strange mingling of the mother's Puritanism and the father's agnosticism bore fruit early is evidenced by the fact that the earliest extant poem of Watson is concerned with the search for God. Confident that he has found God, the youthful poet of about fifteen does not hesitate to share such momentous knowledge with his reader:

> Go to the mountains and the choral woods,
> Or the upheavèd wilderness of sea,
> Or earth's lone wilds and desert solitudes,
> If ye would feel the Mighty Mystery!
> 'Tis there, methinks, is God—where'er the breeze
> Of heav'n wafts incense over wood and field—
> There is the Great Invisible revealed,
> The Soul of Nature's mystic harmonies—
> > Great Nature's self, Ruler of earth and sky,
> > The One Embodiment of Deity.[34]

In typical Victorian fashion, Watson in this sonnet seemed to find a compromise in a kind of Wordsworthian pantheism in which the omnipotence and omnipresence of the Puritan God is fused with the natural forces of the universe. This poem, which Watson never published, later became the basis for "God-Seeking." Still addressing himself to those in search of the Deity, the poet uses the octave to contradict his directions in the earlier poem. It is fruitless, he declares, to seek God "On dawn-lit mountain-tops" and " 'mid thunderous glooms" where "great sunsets burn." Seek Him not, says the poet, in scenes of the natural Sublime, "But where this virgin brooklet silvers past,/ And yellowing either bank the king-cups blow."

In "The Questioner," which interestingly enough contains only a single rhyme sound, the doubtful poet questions the "wondrous trinity" of heaven, earth, and sea about their nature, and they reply that they are "The mask before His face. . . ." After continued questioning, they answer in terms reminiscent of Carlyle: " 'The robe around His form are we,/ That sick and sore mortality/ May touch its hem and healèd be.' " Growing bolder, the questioner asks:

> 'And tell me truly, what is He
> Whose very mask and raiment ye?'
> But they replied: 'Of Time are we,
> And of Eternity is He.
> Wait thou, and ask Eternity;
> Belike his mouth shall answer thee.' [35]

When he completed "The Prince's Quest," Watson evidently felt he had succeeded in writing the kind of poem which would establish his reputation as a poet of great promise. We are told by Helen [Noble] Thomas that before its publication the poet "would stride up and down her father's study, reading alternately passages from Milton and "The Prince's Quest" as if to invite comparison between them." [36] Not only is this interesting glimpse of Watson an indication of just how much he valued his new poem, but it also suggests the kind of poet Watson ultimately wanted to be. Milton had always been to him the poet-prophet par excellence, and the example of Milton—both his life and his work—was to play an increasingly important role in Watson's life as he grew older.

Although this act of pride had nothing to do with Watson's subsequent fall, it is symbolic of the young poet's extreme confidence in his powers as a poet and in the excellence of "The Prince's Quest" in particular. Unfortunately, however, his enthusiasm for the poem and Rossetti's blessing did not guarantee the work's success. In fact, *The Prince's Quest and Other Poems* was a complete failure, and Watson's hopes and expectations were cruelly shattered. Some years later Watson stated that less than twenty copies other than those distributed to friends were sold.[37] Only after the poet reached the heights of fame in the early 1890's was the small first printing exhausted.

For Watson, who from birth had been an extremely high strung, emotionally unstable person, the utter failure of his first volume, and with it the collapse of his hopes and plans for the future, was too much for his sensitive nature to stand. Consequently, the first of his mental crises occurred, and the poet was whisked off to Switzerland and North Africa (with his brother Robinson serving as nurse) to recover.[38] No other event in his long life was ever to be of greater importance to Watson than this mental breakdown. For within these mysterious weeks and months of 1880, the course of Watson's whole life was radically changed and the curve of his poetic development took its one and only decisive turn. When Watson came back to England, he was a new man; and his next volume of poetry, *Epigrams of Art, Life, and Nature* was clearly to indicate a new poet.

Certainly more than just the failure of *The Prince's Quest* volume is the basis for so swift, dramatic, and decisive a change of direction. Several other causes can be suggested. Although Watson did not marry until 1909, he was always particularly susceptible to feminine charm. The love poems in his first volume—"Love's Astrology," "Three Eternities," "Love Outloved," in addition to "Angelo"—suggest that Watson may have had a love affair prior to 1880 which ended unhappily.[39]

Of more genuine significance is the fact that Watson's sympathies, like those of Wordsworth, Tennyson, and Arnold, lay with the poetry of the Classical tradition of English verse: the Miltonic tradition with its lofty conception of the poet-prophet, its notion of high seriousness, and its insistence upon a carefully wrought, consciously perfected art. Like that of his great predecessors, Watson's world-shy, artist's temperament indulged itself for a while in a kind of "pure poetry" based on a lyrical, melancholy, other-worldly impulse; and, in so doing, he was, in his own way, merely following the ideal Classical pattern of the developing poet. After all, his great ideal, Milton, began with pastoral poetry and imitated the "pleasing sound" of the "smooth elegiac poets." Similarly, Tennyson had written his "Recollections of the Arabian Nights" and indulged his "artist's mood" in "The Hesperides" before he forsook his Palace of Art. And like Watson's great exemplars who turned away from their early Romantic effusions toward a poetry "more doctrinal and exemplary" to the nation,[40] he, too, found it imperative to turn his gaze away from himself toward humanity, to an *engagé* poetry chastened, controlled, and perfected in both form and content. This curve of development which occurs in both the life and work of the poets mentioned is, of course, typical not only of Victorian poets and writers such as Tennyson, Carlyle, and Matthew Arnold; it is characteristic of all those who like Milton attempted lighter themes and modes of expression before they matured intellectually and artistically and moved on to themes and genres in keeping with their more objectively oriented point of view.

Although Milton gives no evidence of having moved toward an engaged literature because he needed to lose himself in work and interests outside his psyche, Wordsworth, Tennyson, Carlyle, Arnold—and many others of the nineteenth century—were moved toward a literature of humanity more from fear of self and the imaginative depths of their introspective souls than from any real and powerful desire to right present wrongs. The impulse which led Milton to leave the pastoral and move toward the epic came from that ideal vision in his mind of "a noble and puissant nation rousing herself like a strong man after sleep, and shaking her invincible locks." [41] But work though they did toward solving the gigantic problems of their day, many of the writers of the nineteenth century were moved first by a fear of where excessive self-consciousness would lead. Watson's growth was, in this respect as well as in all others, a typical example of this essentially Victorian curve of development. As his mind and art matured, Watson's sympathies and tastes naturally led him toward the poets and ideals of the Miltonic tradition, and this trend was given impetus by the fact that his growing awareness of his emotional instability drove him away from a preoccupation with self toward a more objective kind of art concerned with contemporary problems. The failure, then, of his first volume was merely a kind of catalyst which brought about the new Watson, the Watson who was later to write the elegy on "Wordsworth's Grave" and *The Purple East* sonnets.

Watson only discussed this momentous change in his life twice. One explanation came many years later in that important conversation with Churton Collins. Until he wrote "The Prince's Quest," Watson told Collins, "merely sensuous poetry" appealed to him. But after spending six weeks (the period of his mental crisis in 1880) reading Shakespeare around the clock, so to speak, he had turned and walked henceforth in a new direction; and, for a time, even Keats and Coleridge had seemed "like toys and flimsy candles" to him.[42]

The other reference comes in that interesting autobiographical poem, "To Edward Dowden," which appeared in *Wordsworth's*

Grave and Other Poems in 1890. Taking Dowden's recently published *Life of Shelley* as his point of departure, the poet goes on, in
typical Watson fashion, to give a brief but perceptive poetic description of the essential Shelley:

> Who hardly brooked on his impatient soul
> The fleshly trammels; whom at last the sea
> Gave to the fire, from whose wild arms the winds
> Took him, and shook him broadcast to the world. (I, 148)

Then Watson recalls that first the voice of Shelley and then that of
Keats enthralled him in youth,

> . . . lapping me in high content,
> Soft as the bondage of white amorous arms.
> And then a third voice, long unheeded—held
> Claustral and cold, and dissonant and tame—
> Found me at last with ears to hear. It sang
> Of lowly sorrows and familiar joys,
> Of simple manhood, artless womanhood,
> And childhood fragrant as the limpid morn;
> And from the homely matter nigh at hand
> Ascending and dilating, it disclosed
> Spaces and avenues, calm heights and breadths
> Of vision, whence I saw each blade of grass
> With roots that groped about eternity,
> And in each drop of dew upon each blade
> The mirror of the inseparable All.
> The first voice, then the second, in their turns
> Had sung me captive. This voice sang me free.
> Therefore, above all vocal sons of men,
> Since him whose sightless eyes saw hell and heaven,
> To Wordsworth be my homage, thanks, and love. (I, 149)

It was the Shakespeare who saw beauty in terror and the Wordsworth who laughed his weak self, his introspective self to scorn in
"Resolution and Independence," and found comfort in "thoughts
that spring/ Out of human suffering," who sustained and reoriented William Watson and gave him the courage to say, "Yea!"
    The two succeeding groups of poems, *Epigrams of Art, Life,*

> And of those who have sung of the magical sea
> Envestured in glory and gleam;
> Of the sea in its languor of passionless calm
> Or in rapture of tempest supreme.

The Romantic themes, moods, and mental states represented in these early poems were later to contrast sharply with the more Classical, objectively oriented *engagé* poetry which Watson was to write after his sudden, rather startling revulsion from the introspective life of the isolated artist after 1880.

In the same year in which his first two poems appeared, 1876, the Watson family moved to Southport, a town on the Irish Sea about twenty-five miles north of Liverpool. Here Watson, now eighteen, began a three-year term of schooling under the direction of a Reverend Mr. Hall, "who kept a day school in Gloucester Road, Birkdale." The reminiscences of a schoolmate afford us a rare close-up of the poet during these rather obscure years. Watson, who evidently never had any interest in outdoor sports, gave all his attention to books at the school where his major concern "was almost exc[l]usively with his own quick mind, which astonished his companions by its skill in dialectic and the fertility of its ideas." Watson, who solved all the scholar's problems with the greatest of ease, appeared to his fellows to do his "homework" during his short walks to and from school. The fierce pride and somewhat haughty bearing of the later poet were clearly beginning to show themselves at this time and were attributed to his "uncommon self-retentiveness." Although he was "aware of his unusual gifts," his fellows were of the opinion that Watson held them "in great control." [19]

Although Watson was now living at some distance from his literary friends in Liverpool, his contact with them did not cease; and he continued to see much of James Ashcroft Noble who urged him on to greater things. Since both men were now very much taken with the Pre-Raphaelite poets, especially with Dante Gabriel Rossetti and William Morris,[20] it is not surprising to find Watson imitating Rossetti in an unpublished sonnet, "The Triple Lordship," which is very much after the manner of *The House of Life* sonnets. Despite its commonplace phraseology and its obscurity, the theme—the preoccupation with Life, Death, and Love—is Rossetti's.

Three spirits rule this earth and all hereon.
The first is Life, the last is doomful Death;

. . . .

But midway twixt these twain the second stands,
And evermore he sings clear songs, and plays
Upon the lute he holdeth in his hands:
Low voice and sweet he hath as any dove;
And who would learn his name needs only gaze
Up at his eyes, wherein is written *Love*.[21]

As August 2, 1879, approached, the date on which he legally
would come of age, Watson must have longed for some wider recognition of his talents than fame had heretofore afforded him. Although two of the Spenserian stanzas from his poem, "Ode on the
Fiftieth Anniversary of the Death of Beethoven," had appeared
in the London *Graphic* in 1877,[22] he was still an unknown poet.
And despite his shyness and introspective tendencies, Watson
had ambition which manifested itself as a burning desire to gain
a position of importance and consequence in the world. It was,
he no doubt felt, the time to come of age poetically as well as legally and to make a bid for national recognition. Meager though
his published work was, it was enough—combined with Noble's encouragement and Watson's thirst for recognition—to lure
him out upon that enigmatic yet tempting "thorny path of fame."
Consequently, he gathered his strength, buoyed up his hope, and
fired his courage for the great attempt to gain a place in the world
of English poetry.

III *"The Prince's Quest"*

First Watson surveyed the field of contemporary poetry and
came finally to look with a good deal of interest on the vogue William Morris had established with his long, pseudo-medieval narrative poems. Although Watson had never attempted anything of
length, he and Noble no doubt felt that a long poem which took
advantage of the current fashion would be a good risk. Besides,
the lengthy narrative would give Watson ample opportunity to
display his poetic talents to the full and, at the same time, allow
him to indulge his taste for Romantic scenes and moods set in
ages and climes remote from the mid-Victorian world of ugly cities and philistine money-makers. Since the venture meant every-

thing to Watson, there can be no doubt that he put all his energies into it. Although little is known about his activities during the two years prior to the publication of his first volume in 1880, there can be little doubt that he was hard at work on a long narrative poem, "The City of Youth: A Faery Romance," later to be called "The Prince's Quest." In the summer of 1879, Watson traveled to the Lake Country, a rural spot replete with atmosphere, valued associations, and cherished memories of his beloved Wordsworth. Instinctively he had turned to the Lakes of Cumberland and Westmorland when, as summer came, he felt his imagination and inspiration failing him. Settled at Broadgate Villa, Grasmere, by July 15, he wrote a rather amusing epistle in verse to James Noble, a letter in which he not only revealed his preoccupation with "The Prince's Quest," but also exhibited his warm vein of gentle humor and his generous and kindly feelings for the man who had done so much for him:

> Dear Noble,—Pray excuse your brother-bard
> For his neglect of writing. It is hard—
> At least I find it so, and always did—
> To sit down to one's writing-desk amid
> A land that makes you covet, in fine weather,
> An out-of-door existence altogether,
> Such as the winds upon the mountains lead,
> Blissful, who write not, neither do they read.
> However, I have got me to my pen
> At last, thank God! So pray, how are you? (When
> You write, don't fail herein to enlighten me.)
> And how are Essie and the bairnies three,
> (The charming last one in particular,
> My baby) and all the world of which you are
> The centre?—Has your beard made any progress
> Since I beheld its nascent splendours? ("Ogress"
> Is the only rhyme that I can think of here,
> And that I must admit looks rather queer
> And just a little foreign to the purpose;
> But bards, you know, should rhyme as linnets
>   chirp, whose
> Chirping is even its own law and knows
> No rules but what its sweet self doth impose:
> At least we have been told so, many times,

By gentlemen who lay down rules for rhymes.)
But I digress. And now I think of it,
What sonnets, essays, epics, have you writ,
During my ten days' absence?—By the bye,
Speaking of literary matters, I
Brought the undying Prince's Quest—(it weighs
Nine ounces, not including leather-case)—
To Lakeland, with intent to add thereto,
Ere I return to Lancashire and you.
Howbeit I have not done a line; for though
I did anticipate an extra flow
Of downright genuine inspiration, somehow
The lyric soul within me has lain dumb. (How
Long it will so continue, there's no judging,
But Pegasus has given no signs of budging,
So far: and I am getting rather tired
Of waiting every day to be 'inspired.')
However I must stop. For as I write
(6.5.P.M.) The sky is waxing bright
Which all the afternoon has grieved in rain:
Under which circumstances I am fain
To leave this barren task of spinning rhyme
And snuff the meadow-airs till suppertime,
In the soft hours that know not any hot sun.
So farewell for the present.—William Watson.[23]

Soon after this letter was written, Watson's inspiration did return, and he was able to finish "The Prince's Quest" during his twenty-first year. The little-known poet, who naturally enough found it impossible to sell his manuscript to a publisher, persuaded his father to provide funds for the publication of the long poem and several shorter ones. Despite his opposition to his son's poetic pursuits, John Watson took his son to London and made arrangements with Messrs. Kegan and Paul to publish the manuscript.[24] In due course, therefore, Watson's first volume, *The Prince's Quest and Other Poems* appeared in April of 1880 bound in khaki cloth boards lettered in gold and decorated in black. It was a handsome little volume in which "The Prince's Quest" appeared first and was followed by a shorter narrative poem, "Angelo," nine lyrics, and four sonnets. "The Prince's Quest," the poem on which Watson's hopes rested, is a long narrative poem of 1814 lines, chiefly in loose couplets divided into ten parts with three lyrics interspersed.

The poem, like the poems of his apprenticeship, is a highly derivative work showing the influences of Shelley and Keats, Wordsworth and Coleridge, Tennyson, Milton, and, in particular, Morris. It, like so many of Watson's works, is fairly bristling with echoes, motifs, and the diction of the poets he loved. In fact, the poem is so highly of a derivative nature that it has been difficult for its critics to agree on any one main influence. One says Shelley; another, Keats; and some, Morris. An early reviewer for the *Academy* sought to solve the dilemma by saying that "The Prince's Quest" is told "in pleasant enough Chaucerio-Keatsio-Morrisian verse." [25] Certainly the "Morrisian verse" is here. Watson's loose handling of the heroic line is close to Morris' use in *The Earthly Paradise*. The pseudo-medieval character of the poem—the quest motif, the mage, the enchanted palaces, the magic jewels, the idealistic Prince himself—is modelled after Morris' then famous and widely read romances. Furthermore, the diction, the tone, and the movement of the verse seem to me to be highly reminiscent of Morris' technique.

The poem commences, as one might expect, with a description of a golden world of long ago, a kind of earthly paradise which existed before the world "fell to waxing gray with weight of years/ And knowledge, bitter knowledge, bought with tears,—" The opening lines, beginning with the Wordsworthian echo, "There was a time," describe a dreamy world of innocence

> When it did seem as if the feet of time
> Moved to the music of a golden rhyme,
> And never one false thread might woven be
> Athwart that web of worldwide melody. (II, 131)

The center of the reader's attention, the Prince, who has grown to manhood in this lovely land, is of a nature and sensibility more rare and ethereal than the Hesperian-garden world of his birth. Like Shelley's poet in *Alastor*, he is the typical romantic youth living in, yet not quite a part of, his world. Handsome, yet delicate,

There lurked at whiles a something shadowy
Deep down within the fairness of his face;
As 'twere a hint of some not-earthly grace,
That made this mortal stripling rather seem
The very dreaming offspring of a dream
Than human child of human ancestry:
So hid in moods fantastical was he
Full often! (II, 132)

Like Tennyson's Prince in *The Princess* who often could not distinguish the "shadow from the substance" and "on a sudden in the midst of men and day" found himself moving "among a world of ghosts," Watson's ascetic youth, too, moves about "likest one" who seems "half-sunk in trance,/ That wanders groping in a shadowy land,/ Hearing strange things that none can understand" (II, 140).

For every handsome prince, there must be a princess; and, having seen her in a strange dream-vision, the hero is forever after in love with her. After some dreamy procrastination, he sets out in search of this lady, who—like the object of the poet's love in *Alastor*—is the embodiment of "all of wonderful or wise or beautiful, which the poet, the philosopher or the lover could depicture." [26] Like that of Keats's Endymion and many another idealistic youth's, his quest for his ideal is a long, often painful, frustrating one which takes him into many strange lands and across many a wild, tempestuous sea before he achieves union with his lady.

There has been some question as to Watson's intentions in his first and only long narrative poem. For instance, Richard Holt Hutton, perhaps thinking of the poem in terms of Shelley's *Alastor* or of Keats's *Endymion,* interpreted it as a kind of allegory, a tale which concerns the "ultimate triumph of the inward vision over the outward hindrances." [27] However, Watson, himself, specifically repudiated this opinion. In a conversation with Churton Collins, he once said that he was "too much under the spell of mere sensuousness to invest it ["The Prince's Quest"] with such an allegory as Hutton found in it; . . ." [28]

Despite this apparent difference of opinion, it seems to me that both Watson and Hutton were correct. Although Watson's primary purpose in writing "The Prince's Quest" was, of course, to produce a mature, finished poem which would establish his claim to fame, he no doubt enjoyed an opportunity to indulge his gift for writing sensuous, mellifluous verse and to exercise his "fancy" by drawing out of his marvelous memory almost at will the various harmonies, voices, archaisms, images, and themes of the poets from Milton to Morris whom he loved.

Besides this primary motive, Watson had no other intention than to write a long, dreamy narrative with no purpose but to soothe and entertain his readers and himself, to lull them away with him from a dull, drab, painfully real world of the present to a golden world of the past where wonders occur often and youth and love are eternal. There is no evidence of a moral theme in "The Prince's Quest"; and there is no indication, such as one finds in *Alastor*, or *Endymion*, or "The Lady of Shalott," that the Romantic idealist is wrong when he turns totally away from humanity to indulge his sensitive soul in an ideal world. Thus, Watson was not only close to Morris in the way he handled the heroic line and shaped the movement of his verse; he was in his intention, also, as close as Morris ever came to a real art for art's sake position. After all, what better description of the young Watson and his intentions in "The Prince's Quest" can be found than Morris' own lines prefaced to *The Earthly Paradise:*

> Dreamer of dreams, born out of my due time,
> Why should I strive to set the crooked straight?
> Let it suffice me that my murmuring rime,
> Beats with light wing against the ivory gate,
> Telling a tale not too importunate
> To those who in the sleepy region stay,
> Lulled by the singer of an empty day.

Watson, then, was right when he said that his poem was the result of an effort to write a merely "sensuous" poetry devoid of any moral or esoteric meaning. But whether he was conscious of it or not, his Prince did represent the subjective, world-shy element in his soul—the romantic Watson of "Time and Tide" and of "World-Strangeness." Watson in these years prior to 1880 was certainly at one with the Prince who walked through a world which seemed "remote and unfamiliar," an alien world in which he, himself, seemed "a something from afar,/ Looking at men as shadows on the wall/ And even the veriest shadow among them all" (II,

164). When his idealistic young Prince refuses the responsibilities of his father's realm and goes in search of a timeless world where beauty and love never fade, Watson was, unconsciously painting a portrait of himself as a young artist.

The enthusiasm of Watson and Noble for Dante Rossetti's poetry naturally led the poet to send a copy of his first volume to the famous man who was living at Tudor House in Chelsea. Watts-Dunton, the companion of Swinburne, once recalled that he saw a copy lying on a table in Rossetti's house and urged the poet to read it. According to his brother William, Rossetti was "immensely taken with it, read passages aloud to me, and predicted great things of the young poet." [29] There is no doubt but what Rossetti was very much impressed by *The Prince's Quest and Other Poems*, for he not only despatched a letter of acknowledgment to Watson, but also wrote to Hall Caine saying that the young poet "must not be discouraged . . . with his real and high gifts." [30] Moreover, after Rossetti's death, his annotated copy of the title poem came into the hands of William Sharp who called attention to Rossetti's "markings and marginalia" and to his special liking for the passage in Part Six in which the mysterious "palace builded of black marble" is described. [31]

The reviews of *The Prince's Quest and Other Poems* were disappointingly few, and none shared Rossetti's enthusiasm. The reviewer for the *Academy*, for instance, found the volume to be run-of-the-mill poetic fare. The verse, which he felt was of a kind all too common at the time, was "tinged with the prevailing affectation of archaic language." [32] The reviewer for the *Athenaeum* also found "The Prince's Quest" to be "somewhat disfigured by affectations of diction," but he went on to say that Watson "has, on the whole, done good work." In addition to declaring that Morris' *The Earthly Paradise* was the chief influence on "The Prince's Quest", he pointed out that Watson was "most original and altogether at his best in those portions of his poem which give greatest scope to imagination." [33]

Among the "other poems" in *The Prince's Quest* volume is "Angelo," another narrative tale with a medieval setting. Consisting of 315 lines of pedestrian blank verse, it tells a somber, unhappy tale of an old but kindly nobleman destroyed by the hatred and falseness of his fair, young wife. Of more interest are three poems which—like Keats's "Ode to a Nightingale" and many another Romantic poem—dramatize the poet's return from a moment of transcendent vision to the harsh world of reality. In "Vanishings," a sonnet, the octave is a simile in which the poet is like one who having looked upon a splendid, fiery world transformed by the setting sun suddenly turns eastward and "Sees a lacklustre world all chill and gray." In the sestet, his dream world vanishes, and he beholds ". . . the dreamless world anew:/ Sad were the fields, and dim with splendours gone/ The strait sky-glimpses fugitive and few" (II, 208).

The lyric, "A Sunset," is similar to the octave of "Vanishings" in that a city is dreaming in the glorious fire of a gorgeous sunset. But the city, too, like the idealist poet, awakes, "Her mighty Fire-Dream o'er," and looks about "amazed, immobile, dumb." The poet again dreaming in the sonnet "Skyfaring" is caught up by the charioteer, Imagination, into his "glistering car." Then

> From shade to shade the wingèd steeds did leap,
> And clomb the midnight like a mountain-sleep;
> Till that vague world where men and women are,
> Ev'n as a rushlight down the gulfs afar,
> Paled and went out, upswallowed of the deep.

But like Keats in "Sleep and Poetry," Watson is unable to sustain the vision and to follow the "ethereal charioteer" for long: ". . . wakened by ten thousand echoes," he suddenly finds "That far-off planet [earth] lying all-too near."

Watson's early attitude toward God is revealed in two poems in the volume, "The Questioner" and "God-Seeking," which reflect a rather typical Victorian state of mind—the conflict between Puritanism and agnosticism. Despite his father's unbelief, the poet as a child was thoroughly indoctrinated with mid-Victorian religious notions. That his brother Robinson became a well-known, popular evangelist is proof enough of the mother's sturdy religious influence. Consequently, as Watson grew older, his will and desire to believe in God, thwarted by the rational evidence of the mind, led him, like so many of his contemporaries, into a frustrating state of doubt, questioning, and indecision which was never completely relieved.

That the strange mingling of the mother's Puritanism and the father's agnosticism bore fruit early is evidenced by the fact that the earliest extant poem of Watson is concerned with the search for God. Confident that he has found God, the youthful poet of about fifteen does not hesitate to share such momentous knowledge with his reader:

> Go to the mountains and the choral woods,
> Or the upheavèd wilderness of sea,
> Or earth's lone wilds and desert solitudes,
> If ye would feel the Mighty Mystery!
> 'Tis there, methinks, is God—where'er the breeze
> Of heav'n wafts incense over wood and field—
> There is the Great Invisible revealed,
> The Soul of Nature's mystic harmonies—
> Great Nature's self, Ruler of earth and sky,
> The One Embodiment of Deity.[34]

In typical Victorian fashion, Watson in this sonnet seemed to find a compromise in a kind of Wordsworthian pantheism in which the omnipotence and omnipresence of the Puritan God is fused with the natural forces of the universe. This poem, which Watson never published, later became the basis for "God-Seeking." Still addressing himself to those in search of the Deity, the poet uses the octave to contradict his directions in the earlier poem. It is fruitless, he declares, to seek God "On dawn-lit mountain-tops" and "'mid thunderous glooms" where "great sunsets burn." Seek Him not, says the poet, in scenes of the natural Sublime, "But where this virgin brooklet silvers past,/ And yellowing either bank the king-cups blow."

In "The Questioner," which interestingly enough contains only a single rhyme sound, the doubtful poet questions the "wondrous trinity" of heaven, earth, and sea about their nature, and they reply that they are "The mask before His face. . . ." After continued questioning, they answer in terms reminiscent of Carlyle: "'The robe around His form are we,/ That sick and sore mortality/ May touch its hem and healèd be.'" Growing bolder, the questioner asks:

'And tell me truly, what is He
Whose very mask and raiment ye?'
But they replied: 'Of Time are we,
And of Eternity is He.
Wait thou, and ask Eternity;
Belike his mouth shall answer thee.' [35]

When he completed "The Prince's Quest," Watson evidently felt he had succeeded in writing the kind of poem which would establish his reputation as a poet of great promise. We are told by Helen [Noble] Thomas that before its publication the poet "would stride up and down her father's study, reading alternately passages from Milton and "The Prince's Quest" as if to invite comparison between them." [36] Not only is this interesting glimpse of Watson an indication of just how much he valued his new poem, but it also suggests the kind of poet Watson ultimately wanted to be. Milton had always been to him the poet-prophet par excellence, and the example of Milton—both his life and his work—was to play an increasingly important role in Watson's life as he grew older.

Although this act of pride had nothing to do with Watson's subsequent fall, it is symbolic of the young poet's extreme confidence in his powers as a poet and in the excellence of "The Prince's Quest" in particular. Unfortunately, however, his enthusiasm for the poem and Rossetti's blessing did not guarantee the work's success. In fact, *The Prince's Quest and Other Poems* was a complete failure, and Watson's hopes and expectations were cruelly shattered. Some years later Watson stated that less than twenty copies other than those distributed to friends were sold.[37] Only after the poet reached the heights of fame in the early 1890's was the small first printing exhausted.

For Watson, who from birth had been an extremely high strung, emotionally unstable person, the utter failure of his first volume, and with it the collapse of his hopes and plans for the future, was too much for his sensitive nature to stand. Consequently, the first of his mental crises occurred, and the poet was whisked off to Switzerland and North Africa (with his brother Robinson serving as nurse) to recover.[38] No other event in his long life was ever to be of greater importance to Watson than this mental breakdown. For within these mysterious weeks and months of 1880, the course of Watson's whole life was radically changed and the curve of his poetic development took its one and only decisive turn. When Watson came back to England, he was a new man; and his next volume of poetry, *Epigrams of Art, Life, and Nature* was clearly to indicate a new poet.

Certainly more than just the failure of *The Prince's Quest* volume is the basis for so swift, dramatic, and decisive a change of direction. Several other causes can be suggested. Although Watson did not marry until 1909, he was always particularly susceptible to feminine charm. The love poems in his first volume—"Love's Astrology," "Three Eternities," "Love Outloved," in addition to "Angelo"—suggest that Watson may have had a love affair prior to 1880 which ended unhappily.[39]

Of more genuine significance is the fact that Watson's sympathies, like those of Wordsworth, Tennyson, and Arnold, lay with the poetry of the Classical tradition of English verse: the Miltonic tradition with its lofty conception of the poet-prophet, its notion of high seriousness, and its insistence upon a carefully wrought, consciously perfected art. Like that of his great predecessors, Watson's world-shy, artist's temperament indulged itself for a while in a kind of "pure poetry" based on a lyrical, melancholy, other-worldly impulse; and, in so doing, he was, in his own way, merely following the ideal Classical pattern of the developing poet. After all, his great ideal, Milton, began with pastoral poetry and imitated the "pleasing sound" of the "smooth elegiac poets." Similarly, Tennyson had written his "Recollections of the Arabian Nights" and indulged his "artist's mood" in "The Hesperides" before he forsook his Palace of Art. And like Watson's great exemplars who turned away from their early Romantic effusions toward a poetry "more doctrinal and exemplary" to the nation,[40] he, too, found it imperative to turn his gaze away from himself toward humanity, to an *engagé* poetry chastened, controlled, and perfected in both form and content. This curve of development which occurs in both the life and work of the poets mentioned is, of course, typical not only of Victorian poets and writers such as Tennyson, Carlyle, and Matthew Arnold; it is characteristic of all those who like Milton attempted lighter themes and modes of ex-

[44]

pression before they matured intellectually and artistically and moved on to themes and genres in keeping with their more objectively oriented point of view.

Although Milton gives no evidence of having moved toward an engaged literature because he needed to lose himself in work and interests outside his psyche, Wordsworth, Tennyson, Carlyle, Arnold—and many others of the nineteenth century—were moved toward a literature of humanity more from fear of self and the imaginative depths of their introspective souls than from any real and powerful desire to right present wrongs. The impulse which led Milton to leave the pastoral and move toward the epic came from that ideal vision in his mind of "a noble and puissant nation rousing herself like a strong man after sleep, and shaking her invincible locks." [41] But work though they did toward solving the gigantic problems of their day, many of the writers of the nineteenth century were moved first by a fear of where excessive self-consciousness would lead. Watson's growth was, in this respect as well as in all others, a typical example of this essentially Victorian curve of development. As his mind and art matured, Watson's sympathies and tastes naturally led him toward the poets and ideals of the Miltonic tradition, and this trend was given impetus by the fact that his growing awareness of his emotional instability drove him away from a preoccupation with self toward a more objective kind of art concerned with contemporary problems. The failure, then, of his first volume was merely a kind of catalyst which brought about the new Watson, the Watson who was later to write the elegy on "Wordsworth's Grave" and *The Purple East* sonnets.

Watson only discussed this momentous change in his life twice. One explanation came many years later in that important conversation with Churton Collins. Until he wrote "The Prince's Quest," Watson told Collins, "merely sensuous poetry" appealed to him. But after spending six weeks (the period of his mental crisis in 1880) reading Shakespeare around the clock, so to speak, he had turned and walked henceforth in a new direction; and, for a time, even Keats and Coleridge had seemed "like toys and flimsy candles" to him.[42]

The other reference comes in that interesting autobiographical poem, "To Edward Dowden," which appeared in *Wordsworth's*

Grave and Other Poems in 1890. Taking Dowden's recently published *Life of Shelley* as his point of departure, the poet goes on, in typical Watson fashion, to give a brief but perceptive poetic description of the essential Shelley:

> Who hardly brooked on his impatient soul
> The fleshly trammels; whom at last the sea
> Gave to the fire, from whose wild arms the winds
> Took him, and shook him broadcast to the world. (I, 148)

Then Watson recalls that first the voice of Shelley and then that of Keats enthralled him in youth,

> . . . lapping me in high content,
> Soft as the bondage of white amorous arms.
> And then a third voice, long unheeded—held
> Claustral and cold, and dissonant and tame—
> Found me at last with ears to hear. It sang
> Of lowly sorrows and familiar joys,
> Of simple manhood, artless womanhood,
> And childhood fragrant as the limpid morn;
> And from the homely matter nigh at hand
> Ascending and dilating, it disclosed
> Spaces and avenues, calm heights and breadths
> Of vision, whence I saw each blade of grass
> With roots that groped about eternity,
> And in each drop of dew upon each blade
> The mirror of the inseparable All.
> The first voice, then the second, in their turns
> Had sung me captive. This voice sang me free.
> Therefore, above all vocal sons of men,
> Since him whose sightless eyes saw hell and heaven,
> To Wordsworth be my homage, thanks, and love. (I, 149)

It was the Shakespeare who saw beauty in terror and the Wordsworth who laughed his weak self, his introspective self to scorn in "Resolution and Independence," and found comfort in "thoughts that spring/ Out of human suffering," who sustained and reoriented William Watson and gave him the courage to say, "Yea!"

The two succeeding groups of poems, *Epigrams of Art, Life, and Nature* and "Ver Tenebrosum," clearly indicate that a new Watson was at work. In his epigrams, the poet is concerned with creating an objective, almost purely impersonal, controlled, and perfected art; and in the political sonnets, "Ver Tenebrosum," Watson handles for the first time a subject based on current public affairs.

IV Epigrams of Art, Life, and Nature

Soon after his return to England in 1880, Watson must have begun a study of the epigram which was merely a prelude to trying his hand at this chastened verse form. As early as November, 1882, a group of his epigrams began to appear in the *Academy,* and groups of ten or twelve continued to be published there through July, 1883. Later in this year, the poet gathered these together, added enough newly composed epigrams to make a total of one hundred, and published them as *Epigrams of Art, Life, and Nature* in January, 1884. The attractive little book was published in Liverpool by Gilbert G. Walmsley.

In a sense the epigrams are purely disciplinary exercises designed by Watson to curb his Romantic and lyrical tendencies. In his "A Note on Epigram" which he appended to the volume, Watson makes it clear that he thinks of the lyric as the exact opposite of the epigram. The "lyrical temper," as it is found, for instance, in Shelley, he wrote, "has little in common with the bent towards Epigram; and thus we are not unprepared to find that the least lyrical of modern English poets of the front rank, Walter Savage Landor, was our greatest modern Epigrammatist." [43] Landor, then, rather than Shelley was now Watson's mentor; the epigram rather than the lyric was now his main interest. His brief but concise and knowledgeable discussion of the history and development of the epigram in the "Note" is evidence enough that he undertook to make a complete study of the form before he decided to devote himself to "the nobler sort of Epigram" which derives from the Greek use of it first as an inscription and then later as "a short poem in Elegiacs, with the qualities of simple beauty and conciseness appropriate to lapidary or monumental uses." Since he found Landor to be the greatest modern epigrammatist in English, Watson set about to learn to write verse which exhibited the qualities he admired in Landor's epigrams: ". . . perfection of simple verse-craft, unshadowed lucidity of phrase, and completeness of utterance." [44]

Along with the emergence of the epigram as a major form in Watson's canon, there also came to light his gift for criticism. In fact, his considerable ability to seize upon the essence of a poet's nature and art demanded a form in which the critical insight could be fully expressed with utmost economy and precision. Since his later poetry shows an almost instinctive use of epigrammatic statement—especially in his handling of the quatrain—it can hardly be denied that Watson, whether he knew it at the time or not, found in the epigram a vehicle intimately suited to his nature and needs.

Just how well Watson succeeded in creating an impersonal, carefully wrought poetry is indicated by William Butler Yeats's response to *Epigrams of Art, Life, and Nature.* Impressed primarily by the "deliberate art" of the Epigrams, Yeats thought of the volume as a "scholar's book." "To know it at all implied almost a knowledge of signs and passwords—membership of some mysterious scholars' Brotherhood of the Rose." The conscious artistry, the perfection, the precision, the cool, impersonal tone of the epigrams so pleased Yeats that he memorized all one hundred poems. To him the *Epigrams* volume remained "more beautiful than any other work of its author's." [45]

Written to demonstrate how purely objective and artist-like he could be, there is no emotion, almost no reflection of self in Watson's epigrams; and often the intricate, carefully wrought art in them is of much more pleasure and interest to the reader than the trite, shallow, commonplace thought and imagery. If any of the various themes are serious statements of Watson's point of view, it is the theme of perfection in art:

> To keep in sight Perfection, and adore
> Her beauty, is the artist's best delight;
> His bitterest torture, that he can no more
> Than keep her long'd-for loveliness in sight. (II, 121)

The poet's tendency to criticize in verse becomes clearly evident for the first time in several of the epigrams. For instance, the

seventh shows extremely well Watson's critical skill and his powers of concise expression:

> Your Marlowe's page I close, my Shakespeare's ope.
> How welcome—after gong and cymbal's din—
> The continuity, the long slow slope
> And vast curves of the gradual violin! (II, 106)

In this volume are not only Watson's mature attitude toward art
and his critical bent, but also his often satirical or ironic brand of
humor which sometimes borders on the bitter. A rather typical
bit of Watsonian sardonic humor is found in "Darwinism Upside-
Down":

> The public voice, though faltering, still demurs
> To own that men have apes for ancestors.
> The inverse marvel fronts me daily, when
> I talk with apes whose ancestors were men.

The reviews of *Epigrams of Art, Life, and Nature* were generally favorable but, like those of *The Prince's Quest and Other
Poems*, were few and slender. J. W. Mackail, writing in the *Oxford Magazine*, gave the volume a very favorable, if brief, recommendation, and found evidences of Rossetti's influence here and
there, especially in Epigrams XX, LXXIV, and LXXXI.[46] H. C.
Beeching, in the *Academy*, felt that Watson's critical epigrams
were not very satisfactory, but he gave the poet a high place in
the long line of practitioners of the art. Of the nineteenth-century
epigrammatists, Beeching ranked Watson alone with Landor.[47]

V Engagé *Poetry: "Ver Tenebrosum"*

Having disciplined himself by achieving perfection of form
within the narrow scope of the epigram, Watson completed his
transformation by turning his attention toward the state of the
nation and its problems. If he were to follow in the footsteps of
Milton, Wordsworth, and Tennyson, the poet knew that he must
not only work toward perfection of form but also concern himself
with a poetry "doctrinal to the nation." Consequently, Watson
ceased to busy himself with the petty problems of fairyland king-

doms and began to occupy himself with the actions of this world. Watson's entry into the sphere of social and political action came in June, 1885, when he published a series of sonnets entitled "Ver Tenebrosum" in the *National Review*, a journal devoted to the Tory point of view and edited by Alfred Austin and William John Courthope.[48] In these political sonnets written in the Miltonic manner, Watson for the first time decks himself in the robes of the poet-prophet and lashes out against his country's unjust actions in the Soudan and against its weak, indecisive response to Russia's hostile moves in Afghanistan.

When these sonnets were written in March and April, 1885, the temper of the nation was at fever pitch and its patience with the Gladstone government nearly at an end. During the previous year, a national hero, General Charles George Gordon had belatedly been despatched to Egypt to establish order, withdraw troops from threatened outposts south of Wady Halfa, and hold the line against the Soudanese who under the leadership of a Mahdi (or Messiah) were taking control of vast areas in the Egyptian Soudan.[49] Soon, however, it became evident that Gordon's mission was, in the words of H. D. Traill, "going to fail: a little longer and it was evident that it had failed; that the emissary who had been sent to 'rescue and retire' was powerless to do either, and was, in fact, himself a prisoner in the city [Khartoum] he had sought to relieve." [50]

For months Gordon was besieged while an army which had been tardily despatched by Gladstone inched painfully up the Nile. The nation waited breathlessly for their hero's emancipation, but to its profound shock and humiliation it never occurred. The general's rescuers reached Khartoum on February 28, 1885, two days after the Mahdists had gained entrance via a gate in the fortress and had shot Gordon to death in the street. No less a personage than Queen Victoria herself was enraged over the catastrophe and sent an angry telegram to Gladstone who, without doubt, had bungled the entire affair from start to finish. During the following months not only was the Egyptian problem more disturbing and unsolved than ever, but the Russians had on March 30, 1885, attacked and cut to pieces an Afghan force defending the key town of Penjdeh on the Afghan-Turcoman frontier. The English did not take this threat to India lightly, and, as

R. C. K. Ensor points out, "for some weeks Great Britain and Russia seemed on the verge of war." [51]

Certainly the circumstances were enough to arouse any poet-prophet worthy of the name, and Watson met the occasion. Choosing the sonnet, a poetic vehicle beloved by the bards of the Miltonic tradition, Watson expressed his feelings in the form consecrated to political use by Milton, Wordsworth, and Tennyson. In doing so, the poet was thoroughly conventional. Throughout the nineteenth century when times of national crisis had occurred, the poets had instinctively turned to the Miltonic sonnet form to express their concern. With Milton's sonnet "On the Late Massacre in Piemont" as their chief guide, Wordsworth in his poems dedicated to National Independence and Liberty; Tennyson in his sonnets, "Montenegro," and "Poland"; and Arnold in "Sonnet to the Hungarian Nation" had proclaimed the tyrant's wrong and had lauded the small, oppressed nations longing for freedom. Thus in Watson's first important appearance as an *engagé* poet, he voiced his attitude toward contemporary events in the form, language, and tone of a well-established tradition. Yeats called the performance "clearly scholars' politics." Watson, he contended, "would have written quite otherwise if Wordsworth and Milton had not written political sonnets before him. The thought and feeling" in these poems "were in no way new or personal, nor are they at any time throughout his poems." [52]

That Yeats was right in thinking that there was no "personal" involvement in the sonnets of 1885 should be questioned, for Watson, always a fiercely patriotic man, demanded the highest conduct of his nation. In the light of his later poetry, it is difficult to believe that the poet in "Ver Tenebrosum" was not sincerely engaged in the issues despite the conventional approach he employed. As one critic was later to point out, "Watson loves England, and longs for her to stand first among nations not only in strength of arms but in lofty principle as well. He writes with more passion of the instances where according to his vision she has disregarded 'her high imperial lot,' than on any other subject." [53]

As fierce as Milton was with the "Owls and Cuckoos, Asses, Apes and Dogs" of his barbarous age, as bold as Wordsworth was in scourging the "Rapine, avarice, expense" of an idolatrous England, neither is more vehement and stern than Watson when in "Ver Tenebrosum" he chastises his country for siding with the forces of tyranny in Egypt. Taking the Radical point of view and urging the English to withdraw and leave the Soudanese free to govern themselves and to choose their own destiny, Watson in "The Soudanese" declares, "They wrong'd not us, nor sought 'gainst us to wage/ The bitter battle." Yet

> . . . when they rose with a gall'd lion's rage,
> We, on the captor's, keeper's, tamer's side,
> We, with the alien tyranny allied,
> We bade them back to their Egyptian cage.

In the two sonnets dedicated to Gordon, Watson is eloquent in praise of the great man. Contemplating the fact that Gordon lies unburied or in an unknown grave, the poet in language reminiscent of Milton's compares him to Moses

> . . . to whom on Nebo's height the Lord
> Showed all the land of Gilead, unto Dan;
> Judah sea-fringed; Manasseh and Ephraim;
> And Jericho palmy, to where Zoar lay;
> And in a valley of Moab buried him,
> Over against Beth-Peor, but no man
> Knows of his sepulchre unto this day. (II, 39)

Perhaps the best known sonnet from "Ver Tenebrosum" is "Our Eastern Treasure," an interesting statement of Watson's attitude toward Imperialism. An answer to those who would allow India to be swallowed by the Russian bear, the sonnet stands as Watson's best effort in the series and as one of the most eloquent apologies for Imperialism in the nineteenth century.

CHAPTER 3

Excursions in Criticism

We cannot believe that he criticiseth best who loveth best all styles both great and small. Surely the best critic is he who, neither ashamed of admiring when he can, nor afraid of reprehending when he ought, does not ask the reader to take his admiration or reprehension on trust, but vindicates both, by adducing such reasons as in all ages have sufficed to demonstrate why masterpieces are masterpieces, and why failures are failures.

—William Watson, "Critics and Their Craft"

INDICATIVE as *Epigrams* and "Ver Tenebrosum" are of Watson's direction after 1880 they do not convey the full impact of the reorientation of William Watson's life and thought. It is in the relatively small but significant body of critical essays and reviews written primarily between 1888 and 1893 and gathered together in *Excursions in Criticism, Being Some Prose Recreations of a Rhymer*[1] that the poet's mature attitude toward literature is for the first time clearly and forcefully enunciated. In these essays, Watson's tendencies toward Classicism (especially his preoccupation with style, form, conscious artistry and his emergence as the *homme engagé* concerned with the condition of England in general and the state of literature in particular are everywhere in evidence. The youthful esthete who once wrote poetry which bore all the marks of Romanticism at its worst is now the mature articulator of a critical doctrine founded upon the principles enunciated by Dr. Johnson and Matthew Arnold.

I *Early Critical Essays*

Although until the late 1880's Watson had been preoccupied with poetry, his emergence as a prose writer and critic had been anticipated by a series of articles on "German Music and the German Musical Composers" contributed to the Liverpool *Argus*,[2] and by a review of Walter Smith's *Kildrostan: a Dramatic Poem* which appeared in the *Academy* in 1884.[3] But it is doubtful if Watson would have devoted so much time and energy to prose had it not been for the sudden death of his father on May 23, 1887. Heretofore relieved of the responsibility of making a living and of maintaining a household, the poet suddenly found himself faced with the necessity of providing not only for himself but also for his semi-invalid mother. In a letter written some years later to the American poet and critic, Louise Chandler Moulton, Watson described his novel situation: "Nine years ago my father, an apparently strong man, died suddenly, and the whole world was changed for me in a moment." [4] Since John Watson had suffered serious financial losses before his death and had left little if anything to his wife and sons, William had no recourse but to turn to criticism for a livelihood. Soon he was contributing essays and reviews to various London periodicals, and especially to the *National Review*, the *Illustrated London News*, the *Spectator*, the *Bookman*, and the *Academy*.

As a consequence of this reversal of fortune, Watson emerged in 1888 as a critic determined to champion all that the Miltonic tradition had come to stand for in the late Victorian period— above all, perfection of form. As Robert Bridges once wrote, Tennyson had educated his generation "to regard finish not only as indispensable, but as the one satisfying positive quality" in poetry;[5] and Watson no less than Bridges had learned well his lesson from the master. In his criticism he was, if anything, "specially observant of blemishes," and he showed no mercy to those whose works appeared to be ill-formed.

Although the enormous influence and weight of Tennyson's practice resulted in a seemingly stable literary situation for a time, the length of his reign and his approaching death were partial causes of a general sense of restiveness which led to open rebellion as the 1880's drew to a close. As a result, Watson entered the lists at a time which he clearly felt to be an hour of crisis in the literary world. Very much concerned about certain tendencies in modern poetry which seemed to him to destroy it (if not for everyone, at least for all but a very few), Watson as critic was almost totally preoccupied during the five-year period between

1888 and 1893, with the task of attempting to stabilize a situation which he believed to be rapidly deteriorating into chaos.

Reared in an age when the greatest poet was in every sense a very popular one, Watson could see that the modern tendency toward a poetry based upon some esoteric logic of the emotions rather than upon the traditional poetic order of thought and event would, for all intents and purposes, stifle poetry as an important means of conveying moral and ethical truths to a large, representative reading public. Certainly one of the reasons Watson cherished the poetic idiom of the Miltonic tradition is that he felt it to be a kind of universal language transcending all dialects and mutations to which common speech is heir, a language as unchanging and awe-inspiring as the truth it expressed. Poetry without this universal appeal was hardly poetry in the sense that it was the chosen vehicle for the utterances of the poet-prophet. Consequently, one can understand his consternation and dismay over the tendencies toward obscurity of expression and disjointed poetic syntax. The vehemence of his attacks upon the poetry of Robert Browning and of Walt Whitman comes partly from his premonition of where their departures from standard poetic rhetorical practices would lead—to what Graham Hough describes as the emotional (and emphatically non-traditional) logic of Eliot's *The Waste Land,* a pastiche of genres, rhetorical modes, and imagistic fragments that are almost totally incomprehensible to the common reader.[6]

Since Watson, then, desired to preserve a poetic idiom which would continue to minister to the needs of a nation, he vigorously denounced any poet in whose work he could detect any deviation from what he considered to be the norm. He criticized John Donne and Browning, among others, because—by breaking or obscuring the narrative or logical continuity of their poems—they violated the traditional principles of style and poetic rhetoric. He opposed all poets who veered toward an art-for-art's-sake position, such as Ernest Dowson and Arthur Symons, because their poems were devoid of serious ethical content. "The art of dispensing with ideas and rising superior to subject-matter is a very fine art," he recognized in his Preface to Alfred Austin's *English Lyrics*, "but in the end readers grow weary of a vast expanse of

melodious rhetoric in which, year by year, the attenuated thing
that passes for thought becomes more and more an inconstant fen-
fire, dancing and disappearing in a boundless mist of words. They
ask that some life and substance shall inform the poet's speech." [7]

Convinced by this time of the value of the Miltonic tradition,
Watson realized that his best chance for saving literature from a
state of complete anarchy was to uphold the concept of literature
sanctioned by tradition and to re-state and re-establish, if necessary, the critical principles derived therefrom. Throughout his
critical canon Watson's constant appeal is to the universally recognized laws of artistic merit embodied in the criticism of the
tradition and to the great writings themselves from which the
laws were derived. Clearly thinking in Arnoldian terms, Watson
believed that the worth of every literary work should be determined by "testing its merit by the very loftiest standard within
reach—placing it side by side with the very best that has been
done in its kind, and noting with candour the likenesses or differences which such a comparison offers to view." [8]

Finding the state of contemporary literary criticism to be anything but adequate to meet so serious a crisis, Watson, especially
in his reviews of Walter Pater's *Appreciations* and of George
Saintsbury's *Essays in English Literature*, set about to curb the
modern tendency to weaken the critic's authority and to reassert
the right of the critic to chastise the writer who failed to measure
up to the high standards set by tradition.

Tracing the history of criticism in the nineteenth century, Watson, in his essay on "Critics and Their Craft," found that during
the early years there "was a general unanimity of opinion that a
critic was primarily and above all else a judge. He himself never
had any misgivings about that. He wore, with an air of judicial
infallibility, the literary ermine; he grew grey in precedents; and
he got into a habit of regarding authors generally as the accused
in the dock." [9] Thinking primarily of men such as Francis Jef-
frey, John Wilson, and Thomas Macaulay, Watson recognized the
fact that they sometimes had judged wrongly and had articulated
principles later reversed by posterity; nevertheless, these Solons of
the literary world at least held firmly to the belief that their "business was to interpret and administer the literary law, and that
this law, though not suscepible of regular codification—being, in-

deed, unembodied in formal statutes—was yet in spirit clearly deducible from tradition and generally approved usage." [10]

Modern critics, Watson found, preferred to appreciate rather than to judge. Their aim was to find something of value in every work and to expatiate upon these virtues either in a vague, overly subtle language, or in an easy, familiar, at times vulgar, style which was in itself a sign of the very disease that the criticism should have been attempting to remedy. Pater, for instance, whose "critical posture is invariably one of extreme modesty," [11] irritated Watson because he humbly approached his authors with "admiration and sympathy" and occupied himself with seeking out and reverently transmitting to his readers "the essence" of their utterances. Although he did not go so far as to openly condemn Pater, Watson's dissatisfaction with his "creed of universal appreciation" is quite clear. Censure is implicit in Watson's statement that Pater's ambition is "simply to understand and report." And although he declares Pater to be "the subtlest artist in contemporary English prose," the admission carries no approval. Moreover, Pater was not only at fault in his critical approach but also in his use of the language. The "honeyed effeminacy" of Pater's style, his "mere daintiness," [12] was anything but reassuring to Watson, whose desire for virile, dignified prose led him to look with equal disfavor upon the easy, familiar style of Saintsbury.[13]

Since the critics had "ceased to assume the role of public censor" and had failed to take seriously their role as "guardians of law and order in literature," [14] Watson made a determined effort to reverse this trend by invoking the pose and spirit of the earlier critic-judges. Certain that his critical principles were sound, Watson in his reviews never allowed anything to deter him from delivering "the maximum sentence" when "eminent offenses against good taste and good sense" were committed. And although he made it clear that it took a good deal of self-control "to go through the performance of such an unpleasant judicial duty," [15] one can readily see that he often delivered his "judicial" opinions with an unusual amount of gusto.

One of the best statements of Watson's critical principles is his essay "The Mystery of Style," which appeared in the *Atalanta* for February, 1893, and was reprinted in *Excursions* shortly thereafter. Dominated by an Arnoldian love for the calm, the decorum, the moderate temper of Greek art, and by his admiration for Milton's "high and flawless excellence," Watson describes Style, this illusive but supreme quality of art, as "high breeding . . . a lofty bearing, inherited from select and distinguished progenitors; and it is essentially the same quality that we admire in the verse of Milton." [16] Although serenity is one of its essential characteristics, a "certain touch of *hauteur* is perhaps inseparable from Style in its most impressive manifestations." In all of this one can see that Watson, as well as Arnold, thought of Style as character—a reflection of its author's nobleness of mind and moral poise.

II *On Modern Poetry*

Surveying the contemporary literary scene, Watson found most disturbing the evidences on every hand that the average intelligent reader, once the backbone of solid literary taste, was exhibiting a shocking lack of discretion. In his essay "Mr. Meredith's Poetry," he deplored the "leniency" of moderns "towards opacity of thought and tortuosity of style";[17] and in a discussion of Emerson's anthology *Parnassus,* he attacked "the modern fallacy" held by many of his contemporaries "that art which gropes for something in the dark is valuable in proportion to the preciousness of the thing groped for, independent of the degree of success which rewards the groper." [18]

Of all the "gropers" in modern poetry, Watson belabored Robert Browning most. This perpetuator of the rough, indecorous tradition of Donne in the Victorian period was, of course, to Watson a real bane. Recognizing Browning's extraordinary ability to understand human nature, Watson nevertheless felt that Browning lacked the other necessary requirement of an artist—the ability to express fully his insights and perceptions of truth. And it was not so much an inability on the part of Browning to develop the capacity to embody his thoughts in clear, precise poetic terms as it was a perverse disregard of the traditionally sound means of poetic communication.

For a time Watson took comfort in the fact that Browning's poetry was not accepted by the large majority of readers. "Yes, Sir," declared his Dr. Johnson in an imaginary conversation in the Elysian Fields with a Victorian inquisitor, "Browning could read men. The pity is, men cannot read Browning." [19] And although it infuriated Watson, he nevertheless was comforted by the fact that, if Browning were admired at all, it was by a small, eccentric cote-rie, a group of intellectual snobs who made a fetish out of poetic perversity and who worshipped obscurity for obscurity's sake. But as the Victorian age waned, not even Watson could overlook the fact that poets like Browning and novelists such as George Meredith were being read by a large and representative audience —a realization which led the critic to remark: "Had Browning's poetry appeared in any other critical age than our own, the best-accredited judges would have said, 'This writer has not mastered the elementary art of making his meaning plain: he expects *us* to disentangle the threads which he himself declines to take the trouble of unravelling for us'—but," continues Watson in a some-what exasperated tone of voice, the readers of today "patiently plod through jungles of contorted and tormented language, and seem rather to enjoy the exercise." [20]

But there was another source of obscurity in poetry which seemed to Watson to be even more dangerous and unwholesome than that found in Browning. It originated in the decadent state of mind expressed in the poetry of Dante Gabriel Rossetti, Algernon Charles Swinburne, and to a more alarming extent in the work of such esthetic poets as Ernest Dowson, Arthur Symons, and Oscar Wilde. In the poetry of these men, Watson found a loose, lan-guorous style and an effeminate, luxurious language—one insidi-ous in its hypnotic effect and emotional appeal and one devoid of all ideas and meaningful content. This kind of poetry was the most repulsive of all to Watson, and there can be no doubt that he be-lieved it to be a deadly poison which, spreading through society, could weaken it and destroy its will to face life with the moral poise and sturdy purpose with which he was convinced it must be met. Writing in 1890 on the threshold of that last critical decade of Victoria's reign, Watson was confident that

Unless immemorial principles of right taste and judgment are to be annulled, life, substance, reason, and reality, with a just balance of sense and sound, are what future generations will look for in our singers. And surely if poetry is not to sink altogether under the leth-argy of an emasculate euphuism, and finally die surfeited with un-wholesome sweetmeats, crushed under a load of redundant ornament,

and smothered in artificial rose-leaves, the strenuous and virile temper
. . . must come to be more and more the temper of English song.[21]

With much critical insight, Watson turned to Shelley and held
him "responsible for that prevalence of the loosely thought and
the inexactly said which deforms so much of" modern poetry.[22] He
was convinced that the decadent qualities he found in the esthetic poetry of his day were the qualities which the genius of
Shelley "first signally impressed upon our literature." [23] In Shelley's
poetry, as well as in much of the poetry of the 1880's and 1890's,
Watson found "a vertebral weakness, a want of intellectual stamina and staying power; an absence of our older national characteristic of massive and burly rather than agile strength; an effusive-
ness, expansiveness, dilution, which really argue a defective sense
of proportion and form." In the poetry of Swinburne, in particular,
he criticized "a trick of seeming to be always singing in a shrill,
ear-piercing treble." These "thoroughly un-English" elements
were destroying the effectiveness not only of so much modern poetry, but also of society to face responsibilities from a position of
strength. Without "Shelley's imaginative vision, and lyrical passion" to redeem them, the esthetic poets had nothing of any real
value to offer. In his most complete analysis of this kind of poetry,
Watson, speaking again through his Dr. Johnson in the interesting critical parody, "Dr. Johnson on Modern Poetry," discussed
Rossetti's sonnet, "Through Death to Love" (No. XLI) from *The
House of Life,* and found it to be "truly a greater body of non-
sense condensed within fourteen lines than I had believed fourteen lines to be capacious of." [24]

Watson's general dissatisfaction with the poets of his day should
not, however, lead one to believe that he found no poet who approached his standards of clarity, decorum, and perfection of
form. In addition to Tennyson and a number of minor, now-
forgotten poets, Watson found the poetry of Robert Bridges to be
"free from all taint of the literary vices of our time. . . ." Although he praised Alfred Austin's poetry in the Preface to *English
Lyrics,* Watson's preference for the work of Bridges is clear. Of
Bridges' early shorter poems, the critic found the "Elegy on a
Lady" especially beautiful—"Classic in its lovely chastity of style."

It was for him "a faultless piece of art—art, of course, of the self-conscious kind." [25]

In his critical comments on American poetry, Watson generally approved the poetical practices of such poets as Longfellow, Whittier, and, in particular, James Russell Lowell.[26] But, as has been noted, Walt Whitman's works were "entirely unattractive" to him whose conception of literature demanded more respect for the heroic line and poetic decorum than the author of *Leaves of Grass* was prepared to give. Certainly Watson's inability to understand what Whitman in particular and other modern "rebels" in general were doing is revealed by the following remark made in reference to Whitman's poetical practice: "Literature is not the random pouring-out upon paper of all one's feelings and notions, helter-skelter, head over heels, jostling one another on the jumbled page. It is," according to Watson, "a slow distillation from hours and years of sensation and thought. The kingdom of poetry, like that of heaven," he opined, "is not [to] be taken by violence." [27]

In general agreement with Whitman's social ideals and with his response to nature, Watson deplored, however, the poet's frank use of sex in his poems. Reacting against the view that, if literature is life, it cannot ignore the sexual relationship between man and woman, Watson declared that aspects of man's nature such as sex which are shared "in common with hogs and horses, are in no sense proper and special to humanity, and are therefore *not* fit themes for man's art." [28]

There were other themes besides sex which Watson considered unfit for art. And in his critical discussions of the drama, he vigorously opposed morbid, pessimistic representations of life which, as Arnold phrased it, "are painful, not tragic." His main criticism of the dramas of Ibsen and of the Jacobean playwrights is that they, unlike true tragedies, fail—despite all their blood, thunder, and mental anguish—to "inspirit and rejoice the reader." The suffering one contemplates in them finds no vent in meaningful action. Watson recognized Henrik Ibsen to be a writer of great power and genius who failed as a dramatist because he confined his vision to but one side of life. As Watson said, "I am glad to have read Ibsen, if only because he sends me back with a new zest to the masters who saw life steadily, and saw it whole." Unlike Sophocles and Shakespeare who "deal with life," Ibsen, Watson believed, dealt "only with death-in-life. They treat society; he treats only of the rottenness of society. Their subject is human nature—his, human disease." [29]

Sharing Matthew Arnold's abhorrence of dramatic poetry which demoralized rather than inspirited, Watson felt that the theater should show us "men and women in great situations, heroically doing and enduring." But not only was Ibsenism spreading rapidly across Europe, but in England itself there was a school of critics actively engaged in dredging up the Jacobean dramatists such as John Ford and John Webster whose plays no less than Ibsen's painted "a lurid and chaotic world" totally lacking in any moral or spiritual value.[30] Tracing this interest in the Jacobeans back to Charles Lamb, William Hazlitt, and Leigh Hunt, Watson in "Some Literary Idolatries" readily agreed that Marlowe was a great and significant poet, the real founder "both of English tragedy and English blank verse"; but he could not understand these critics' praise of dramatists who do not "feed man's spirit."

As a result, Watson could hardly forgive Lamb and his more recent adherents, such as Swinburne, for reviving an interest in playwrights who were long ago so rightly assigned to oblivion.

Like Dr. Johnson who disapproved of fantastic tales and the "wild strain of imagination" found in Romances because they were too "remote from all that passes among men" for the reader to make "any applications to himself," [31] Watson was on the whole hostile to the use of supernatural elements and of strange, unusual occurrences in literature. Believing that the reader could more easily find ethical value in realistic representations of everyday life and inaccurate portrayals of normal beings, he found it difficult to praise dramas, poems, or novels which exploited the unreal for any purpose. Although he called Coleridge's "The Ancient Mariner" the "finest example in our literature, of purely fantastic creation," Watson felt it to be a successful poem because Coleridge was "careful not to introduce any element of the marvellous or supernatural until he has transported the reader beyond the pale of definite geographical knowledge, and thus left behind him all those conditions of the known and the familiar, all those associations with recorded fact and experience, which would have created an inimical atmosphere." [32]

But poets such as Edgar Allan Poe who dealt constantly in terms of the fantastic yet real world—in a kind of world in which the real could hardly be distinguished from the marvellous—were not, so far as Watson was concerned, healthful poets. "Poe was a literary artist of much power," he remarked in "Some Literary Idolatries," and although "the objects viewed through his poetic lens are seen with a sombreness of body and prismatic brilliancy of outline which are not the shadow and light of nature, yet [they] have their peculiar fascination." But, continued Watson, "the authentic masters, are they not masters in virtue of their power of nobly elucidating the difficult world, not of exhibiting it in a fantastic lime-light?" [33]

III *On the Modern Novel*

This steady opposition of Watson to the unwholesome, exaggerated, unlifelike representations in poetry and drama is also clearly evident in his discussions of the novel. Characteristically, Watson lamented the fact that the "old merits of fulness and 'body'—virtues apparently hereditary in that lineage of robust minds which can be traced backwards without a break from George Eliot to Fielding—have been growing rarer and rarer." In their place, the critic found the novel deteriorating in opposite but equally false directions. On the one hand, the society novel—in particular the "species grown in American soil, or rather in New York conservatories and forcing beds"—had become a marvel of "elaborate triviality which no amount of cleverness can render other than vapid." With Henry James clearly in mind, Watson referred to the contemporary novel of manners as a miracle "of inexhaustible nothingness, in which the tiniest rivulet of incident just trickles across a continent of dialogue." [34] On the other hand, there was the novel of adventure characterized by its details of carnage, horror, ferocity, its improbable actions, and unbelievable coincidences. "From coma," Watson sadly observed, the contemporary novel passes "into convulsions."

It was with these aberrations of the popular adventure novel that Watson first dealt when he turned to criticism in 1888. In his most notorious review, which was published anonymously as "The Fall of Fiction," Watson, careless of the fact of Rider Haggard's tremendous vogue at the moment, accused the author of *King*

Solomon's Mines of cleverly anticipating the decline in public
taste and of encouraging it by issuing novels which were characterized by the "element of the physically revolting"—massacres,
cruelty, bloody death—and by the "element of the fantastic, preternatural, and generally marvellous." Deploring the public's taste
for what he termed "the sham-real and the sham-romantic," Watson likened Haggard's novels to "coarse and violent intoxicants"
which offer the reader mere escape from a reality to which he returns weakened and dispirited.

Like Dr. Johnson whom he quoted throughout the review,
Watson objected to Haggard's "employment of incidents which,
though perhaps not outside the pale of nature, are yet gratui-
tously improbable." [35] In wholehearted agreement with Johnson
that fiction must "exhibit life in its true state, diversified only by
accidents that daily happen in the world, and influenced by passions and qualities which are really to be found in conversing
with mankind," Watson focussed his critical gaze upon Haggard's
unrealistic presentation of life.[36] No less an ethical teacher than
Dr. Johnson, Watson felt that men could only gain the truth from
contemplating and studying situations in life with which they
could identify. Consequently, Haggard's novels could hardly be
vehicles of ethical values even if there were any to be derived
from an absorption in their events.

In a passage which illustrates Watson's rather frequent indulgence in sarcasm, the critic described the climactic moment in
King Solomon's Mines when Quatermain and company at last enter the treasure chamber where "they pass through the Place of
Death, where the corpses of the defunct kings of Kukuanaland sit
with water slowly dripping upon them from the rock ceiling, until
by its agency they are converted into stalactites—a charming
conception." However, nothing but one of Watson's brutally frank
frontal assaults would satisfy him in his remarks on *She*. Pointing
out that it was its author's most popular work, the critic went on to
declare it "the worst, its horrors being the coarsest, its artistic ma-
chinery the most lumbering and creaky, and, altogether, its mon-
strosities the most crudely monstrous that Mr. Haggard's writings
can show." [37]

As if this were not enough, Watson unfortunately went on to
add to his charge of charlatanry the accusation of plagiarism. In

so doing, he provoked a contemptuous reply entitled "A Dip in Criticism" by Andrew Lang.[38] Clearly irked and revolted by what he felt to be the anonymous reviewer's pious, pedantic tone, Lang with irony and sarcasm berated Watson for making serious accusations which could not be answered directly. Accusing an author of plagiarism and then of hiding behind the veil of anonymity seemed to him to be no less than an act of shameful cowardice. Assuming that the anonymous critic was a young novelist jealous of Haggard's extraordinary popularity, Lang attributed the malicious attack to spite and concluded his defense by comparing the reviewer to Bunyan's Mr. Envy.

The following month, Watson came to his own defense in an anonymous reply entitled, "Mr. Haggard and His Henchman." After pointing out (for the benefit of those who did not know) that Haggard and Lang admired each other and that Haggard's *She* was dedicated to Lang, Watson commenced his rebuttal by making fun of the novelist "who kills you a dozen men in a paragraph, and watches their elaborate death-throes with a coolness worthy of our old friend Parrhasius; here is the learned professor of carnage, the unapproachable master of massacre, the unrivalled man-sticker and supreme elephant-potter of fiction, the novelist whose pages are littered with the carcases of his slain— could anybody have supposed that he himself was other than pachydermatous and bullet-proof?" [39]

In "The Fall of Fiction," Watson, as has been seen, was concerned with the contemporary novel of adventure and with its unrealistic, distorted representation of life, and with its reliance on the sensational. A year later in October, 1889, he published his second important discussion of the novel in the *National Review*. In "Fiction—Plethoric and Anaemic," he dealt primarily with the society novel which he found to be in something like a state of pernicious anaemia. But before he turned directly to this problem, he penned a defense of George Eliot in which he again reaffirmed his support for the novel of tradition which relied on realism; on sturdy, representative characters; and on a good story with morally elevating thoughts and actions. Responding to recent adverse criticism of the great lady—especially an attack by Frederic Harrison—Watson was somewhat at a loss to account for the current charge that George Eliot was a writer "in whom 'action is subordinated to reflection!'" Even when one sets "aside the wisdom of life with which" her novels teem, Watson observed, "when one thinks of the opulence of material, the mere mass of story, in such a book as *Adam Bede,* when one thinks of the tragedy of passion and error and fate in it, the exquisite comedy of humours and manners, the play and movement of circumstance, the sweeping tide of event, this wretched gabble about George Eliot," he concluded, is "ineffably silly and inane." [40]

If Frederic Harrison felt that George Eliot's novels subordinated action to thought, one can hear Watson muse: what must he think about the fiction of Henry James and William Dean Howells. "Who that has read the novels of Mr. James and Mr. Howells," he inquired, "can fail to observe how attenuation and depletion are becoming features of modern literature?" Caught in a not unusual moment of glancing backward toward an age which seemed to him so much more vital and alive, Watson, in one of his best passages, asked why it was that

instead of feeling happy . . . in one of Mr. James's aesthetic drawing rooms, among those most superior people to whom he introduces us so gracefully, we find ourselves looking out of window and thinking wistfully of the substantial literary entertainment of our youth, when novelists, like genial hosts, gave us broad hospitality and hearty English fare? . . . Perhaps we are saying to ourselves, Oh, for a ride across country after the hounds with Squire Western! Ay, or a chat about Homer with Parson Adams, over a pot of ale.[41]

Turning from the esthetic drawing rooms of James to the brilliantly mannered world of Diana and Sir Willoughby Patterne of Meredith's *Egoist,* Watson delivered his most extended critique of the anemic novel. And, indeed, it is odd that it was the celebrated novels of the man to whom *Excursions in Criticism* was dedicated which Watson singled out for the most thorough castigation. Speaking of Meredith as "the truest of poets" in his dedication, Watson found Meredith's poetry entirely free from the "incoherence," "verbal obscurity," and "surface-vice of manner" that made the novelist's fiction anathema to him.[42] Always piqued by the extravagant claims put forward on Meredith's behalf by a small group of avid supporters, Watson in "Fiction—Plethoric and Anaemic" did not fail to point out that Meredith had still not

gained popularity among "a representative jury of novel-readers."
Attempting to understand why some persons felt that Meredith's
novels were very great, Watson asked several basic questions
which needed to be answered in the affirmative, if according to
past standards, Meredith's fiction were to be approved. "Is he
great at construction?" the critic inquired. "Is he great as a master
of narrative? Is he great as an artist in dialogue? Is he great as a
creator of character?" And on all of these points Watson was
obliged to answer, *No*.[43]

As one might expect, Watson considered *The Ordeal of Richard Feverel* Meredith's most successful work, the novel which (in
words reminiscent of that eminently practical sage, Jeremy Bent-
tham) "gives the greatest pleasure to the greatest number of readers." In this early work, Watson found a good story told in a clear,
straight-forward manner with none of the needless complexity,
obscurity, and aphoristic pyrotechnics which marred the later
novels. But, unlike Robert Louis Stevenson who found *Rhoda
Fleming* "the strongest thing in English letters since Shakespeare
died," Watson dismissed it as very bad; and he then stated that
"the thinness of the subject-matter" in *Diana of the Crossways*
"may be forgiven in consideration of the frequently glittering dialogue, and the brilliance of the author's asides."

Yet none of these elements of relief could be found by Watson
in *The Egoist*, a novel which he declared to be "the most entirely
wearisome book purporting to be a novel that I ever toiled
through in my life." Unable to evolve his plot in an orderly, natural manner, Meredith had complicated the matter further by his
"perverse reluctance to say a plain thing in a plain way." [44] Concluding his remarks by summarizing Meredith's style, Watson
characterized it as "stiff without dignity and lax without ease; a
style that attempts rapidity, to achieve fuss; a style aggressively
marked and mannered, an intractable style that takes the initia-
tive, leads the way, dominates the situation, when it should be
. . . simply an obedient instrument, a blade to be carved with,
not to be flashed in our eyes." [45]

Despite Thomas Hardy's pessimistic, often terrifying view of
the universe and of the human condition, Watson in one of his
best reviews, "Mr. Hardy's 'Tess of the D'Urbervilles,'" gave the
novelist high praise. Unable to convict Hardy of any of the foibles

of the society novelists, Watson devoted most of his attention to the portrayals of Angel Clare and Tess and to Hardy's arraignment of the universal forces which determine the fate of man. Recognizing that Angel Clare was the most subtly drawn and "in some ways the most perplexing and difficult character in the novel," Watson observed that the reader often felt more anger toward this troubled intellectual than toward Alec d'Urberville.[46]

On but one point did Watson question Hardy's handling of Tess, a point which has continued to bother critics and discriminating readers of the book. "Considering the proud ancestry whose blood was in her veins, and the high spirit and even fierce temper she exhibits on occasion," observed the critic, "one almost wonders at her absolute passivity under such treatment as he [Angel Clare] subjects her; but the explanation obviously lies in her own unquestioning conviction of the justice of his procedure." After all his objections to the novels of James and Meredith, it is good to have Watson so justly observe in his conclusion that "*Tess* must take its place among the great tragedies, to have read which is to have permanently enlarged the boundaries of one's intellectual and emotional experience." [47]

Although Watson's critical output was, comparatively speaking, rather small during the five-year period covered by his *Excursions in Criticism*, the range of these essays provides us with an adequate knowledge of his critical stance and of his attitude toward the major forms of literature. Certainly much that is revealed in the essays is rather disconcerting. The fact that as a critic Watson could praise without reservation the poetic effusions of Madame Darmesteter and Graham R. Tomson's "The Ballad of the Bird-Bride," but condemn in the harshest terms poets such as Donne, Browning, and Whitman is, to say the least, hardly reassuring.[48] Watson's obstinate opposition to his literary contemporaries such as Yeats, Ibsen, and James, who are accepted today as great writers, does not speak well for him as a critic despite the fact that he justly praised George Eliot, Milton, Tennyson, Bridges, and Hardy.

Without doubt, Watson's greatest fault as a critic lay in his inability to recognize great literary works of genius that were expressed in forms and terms other than what he considered to be the traditional ways and means. Seemingly hypnotized by the superficial sound and external mannerisms of the Miltonic poetic tradition, Watson was displeased when a poet outside this tradition dared to publish his work; and he was outraged when this work gained the applause of an intellectual coterie. If poetry did not have the studied smoothness and sentiments of the tradition —its authentic ring—it was simply not, so far as Watson was concerned, poetry. That a poet could express certain valuable states of mind, convey significant truths, and embody complex emotions and responses to experience in what Watson took to be rough, obscure verse thrown together helter-skelter never occurred to him.

But in all of his utterances, Watson was absolutely sincere and true to his convictions. His critical pronouncements ring with the zeal and authentic tones of a man speaking from the heart and convinced also that he is on God's side.

Today Watson's criticism claims attention not so much for any intrinsic value it may contain but because of the historical position it represents. This stance maintained in *Excursions* is an excellent indication of the strength and influence of the Miltonic tradition even at the moment when it was becoming the center of attack by poets and critics who felt it was no longer useful. Watson was but one of many important poets—such as Bridges, Coventry Patmore, and Gerard Manley Hopkins—who continued to find the artistic aims and achievements of the tradition a source of inspiration and guidance. Since they believed it could be modified and extended to meet the needs of the modern world, they were loath to break away entirely from its laws and its idiom. Watson, able to rely on the Miltonic tradition as a standard of merit, upheld for the late Victorians some ideal of order and value in literature at a time when the poets who were rebelling against the *status quo* hardly knew where they were going.

Since Watson failed to see the possibilities for great poetry in the untraditional modes of poetic experimentation being pursued by his now-illustrious contemporaries, he must be condemned as a critic; but, in so far as he recognized that the direction which these experimentations were taking would lead to an esoteric poetic idiom incomprehensible to the vast majority of readers, he must be applauded. For not the least of his worries, as we have seen, was the concern to maintain poetry as a major source of inspiration and truth for mankind as a whole.

CHAPTER 4

In Search of a Singer

> Where is the singer whose large notes and clear
> Can heal, and arm, and plenish, and sustain?
> —William Watson, "Wordsworth's Grave"

SINCE Watson's finest poem, "Wordsworth's Grave," is so clearly the basis of his sudden rise to fame in 1891, I have chosen to discuss it here even though it was completed in 1887 and therefore anticipated the main bulk of Watson's criticism in prose. Begun, appropriately enough, at Rydal in the heart of the Lake District in May, 1884,[1] the poem serves as a link between *Epigrams of Art, Life and Nature* and Watson's mature critical opinions and concerns revealed in his prose and later poetry. Composed of forty-seven heroic quatrains, the elegy's calm, sober, nostalgic tone and its stately, carefully wrought verse form an interesting contrast to the often vehement, excited tone and forceful manner of "Ver Tenebrosum" and much of the prose criticism. Nevertheless, the motive and theme are the same. Preoccupied as in his prose with a contemporary situation which he found very disturbing and distasteful, Watson in "Wordsworth's Grave" was chiefly concerned with the state of poetry at the present time. He criticized the "misbegotten strange new gods of song"; eulogized the authentic, traditional poets of the past; and upbraided the vagrant, faithless souls—his wayward contemporaries.

I *"Wordsworth's Grave"*

That he, like Arnold's Wordsworth, was living in an iron age was the one great fact of Watson's mature years—the irritation, so to speak, which activated and gave direction to his major efforts during his years of affluence. Consequently, the main impulse at this time was critical—one which led Watson to use his powers as a poet and prose writer to lash out alternately against or lament the false direction taken by literature. Certainly the fact that Watson found himself a champion of the old ways, swimming against an irresistible current, largely explains his increasing pessimism, his growing sense of alienation, as well as his impulse to criticize.

The subject, then, of "Wordsworth's Grave" is poetry—a rejection of its present degraded state and an appeal for a singer like Wordsworth who can inspirit a nation. The poem is not so much a lament for Wordsworth as it is a wistful song of longing for the particular kind of poetry he better than anyone else could write. From one point of view Watson's poem's closest analogue is Wordsworth's own "Milton! thou shouldst be living at this hour." Thus the critical and elegiac impulses are mingled and sustained in a poem whose subject and tone are highly reminiscent of Arnold's elegiac poems, especially of his "Memorial Verses." Coming from the shy, world-weary side of Watson, the fifth and central section of the poem[2] is a sincere, moving lament for poetry which "is loth,/ Or powerless now, to give what all men seek!" Voicing the attitude of many perplexed and worn Victorians, Watson rejected the contemporary poetic bill of fare which either "deadens with ignoble sloth/ Or deafens with shrill tumult, loudly weak." Plagued by what Arnold called "this strange disease of modern life,/ With its sick hurry, its divided aims," Watson, like so many of those who responded to his poetry, found "empty music"; Browning's was "heart refreshing" but intellectually tiring poetry of little consolation. And although some poets like Morris went "prankt in faded antique dress,/ Abhorring to be hale and glad and free," and others paraded "a conscious naturalness,/ The scholar's not the child's simplicity," the result was the same—no peace, no help for pain.

Reiterating Wordsworth's charge that modern man had cut himself off from the springs of life and of spiritual power in nature, Watson in Section I of the poem hoped that the vagrant soul of the modern world would not long delay in the paths of prodigality but, "returning to herself/ Wearily wise," would return to a right appreciation and understanding of Wordsworth and

> . . . the powers that with him dwell:—
> Inflowings that divulged not whence they came;

And that secluded Spirit unknowable,
The mystery we make darker with a name.

Commencing the second movement of the elegy with the question: "Poet who sleepest by this wandering wave!/ When thou wast born, what birth-gift hadst thou then?", Watson, exhibiting his ability to accurately define the essential qualities of poets with epigrammatic deftness and poetic grace, continued:

Not Milton's keen, translunar music thine;
Not Shakespeare's cloudless, boundless human
view;
Not Shelley's flush of rose on peaks divine;
Nor yet the wizard twilight Coleridge knew.

Yet men who sought refuge from "blast and blaze,/ Tumult of tottering heavens," turned "From Shelley's dazzling glow or thunderous haze,/ From Byron's tempest-anger, tempest-mirth," to Wordsworth whose poetry was the embodiment of "peace on earth"—

Nor peace that grows by Lethe, scentless flower,
There in white languors to decline and cease;
But peace whose names are also rapture, power,
Clear sight, and love: for these are parts of peace.

Referring again in Section III to the modern poetic plight, Watson lamented the loss of true feeling and heart-felt emotion in poetry since the days of Wordsworth. He contrasted with sarcasm the "wondrous skill" of the present-day "word-mosaic artificer" who can "simulate emotion felt no more" with Wordsworth who sang "A lofty song of lowly weal and dole./ Right from the heart, right to the heart it sprang,/ Or from the soul leapt instant to the soul."

Focussing attention on another age which, much like his own, saw poesy "Put off her robe of sunlight, dew and flame," and don "a modish dress to charm the Town," Watson, in his fourth movement, detailed in typical nineteenth-century fashion the history of poetry between Milton and Wordsworth. Finding the Augustan Age a time of "sterile wit," artifice, and starved emotions, the poet looked beyond the half-truths of a false poetry to see that men, nevertheless, "joyed and wept, and fate was ever new,/ And love was sweet, life real, death no dream." And in his reference to the poetry of Dr. Johnson, it is not surprising that Watson in a bare, epigrammatic statement of four lines strikingly and accurately revealed the qualities which drew him so close to this master:

> In sad, stern verse the rugged scholar-sage
> Bemoaned his toil unvalued, youth uncheered.
> His numbers wore the vesture of the age,
> But, 'neath its beating, the great heart was heard.

Tracing the slow but sure return of authentic verse through the efforts of Collins, Gray, Goldsmith, and Burns, Watson brought the section to a close with the rise of those "Twin morning stars of the new century's song,/ Those morning stars that sang together. . . ."

Taking his lead from the famous delegation of duties, so to speak, referred to in Chapter XIV of the *Biographia Literaria,* Watson characterized Coleridge as the dreamer who "In elvish speech . . . told his tale/ Of marvellous oceans swept by fateful wings"; and described Wordsworth as the seer who

> . . . strayed not from earth's human pale,
> But the mysterious face of common things
>
> He mirrored as the moon in Rydal Mere
> Is mirrored, when the breathless night hangs blue:
> Strangely remote she seems and wondrous near,
> And by some nameless difference born anew.

Certainly the crucial question of the poem occurs in Section V in which Watson, centering his attention on the inability of the modern "lyre" to bring peace to the troubled heart of man, earnestly cried out: "Where is the singer whose large notes and clear/ Can heal, and arm, and plenish, and sustain?"

In a time of social and intellectual upheaval and transition Watson was convinced that poetry had a crucial role to play in the affairs of the nation; and it had an obligation which could best be fulfilled by calming, inspiriting, and reassuring the people instead of aiding and abetting the forces of disintegration and decadence by embodying bizarre states of mind or untried responses to art and life in unfamiliar idioms and in obscure language and forms. As a result, it was no accident that Watson turned to the poetry of Wordsworth as the kind which his age most needed. He knew—no doubt from experience—the healing power of Wordsworth's verse, the sense of placid simplicity and quiet thoughtfulness which nature's own poet could invoke. Standing beside the simple grave close by "The old rude church" whose "bare, bald tower" cast its shadow where "high-born Rotha flows," Watson found the peace and rest which Wordsworth's poetry so often embodied:

> Afar though nation be on nation hurled,
>   And life with toil and ancient pain depressed,
> Here one may scarce believe the whole wide world
>   Is not at peace, and all man's heart at rest.
>
> Rest! 'twas the gift *he* gave; and peace! the shade
> *He* spread, for spirits fevered with the sun.
> To him his bounties are come back—here laid
>   In rest, in peace, his labour nobly done.

Where, then, is the singer whose large notes and clear can heal and arm and plenish and sustain? Here in the serenely melancholy, beautifully modulated music of "Wordsworth's Grave" many a late Victorian found him. With its idealized but compelling vision of the revered poet; its stanza, tone, and imagery of Gray's beloved *Elegy;* and its Arnoldian intellectual aura and sense of wistful resignation, "Wordsworth's Grave" was to many of Watson's day a welcome relief in the midst of wild experimentation and extravagant poetical posing. And it was especially to be a sign of hope and inspiration when Arnold lay in Laleham churchyard and Tennyson was at rest in the Abbey.

Watson's response to Wordsworth in his elegy clearly indicates the source of his devotion to the elder poet. Watson was not, as critics were quick to point out, closely akin to Wordsworth either personally or poetically. As Cosmo Monkhouse phrased it, Wordsworth was Watson's "spiritual king," [3] and this relationship had developed after the poet's infatuation with the poetry of Shelley, Keats, and Rossetti. During his youthful years, Wordsworth's voice impressed Watson as being "Claustral and cold, and dissonant and tame"; consequently, it long went unheeded until that dark day in 1880 when, in the midst of severe depression and mental anguish, Watson discovered the Wordsworthian magic which from

> homely matter nigh at hand
> Ascending and dilating, . . . disclosed
> Spaces and avenues, calm heights and breadths
> Of vision, . . . ("To Edward Dowden," I, 149)

Like John Stuart Mill who in the autumn of 1828 found that "Byron was exactly what did not suit" his condition but that "Wordsworth was exactly what did," Watson discovered what Arnold called "Wordsworth's healing power" in a time of mental crisis. He then went forth a disciple to preach the good news to a similarly afflicted world.

What in Wordsworth's poetry had such a salutary effect on the Victorian mind is detailed in Mill's *Autobiography,* and the striking accuracy with which he pointed out the essential elements is shown by its close correlation with Watson's delineation many years later in "Wordsworth's Grave." Finding no help in Wordsworth's most Victorian poem, *The Excursion,* Mill had turned to the two-volume edition of 1815 in which he found poems which "addressed themselves powerfully to one of the strongest of my pleasurable susceptibilities, the love of rural objects and natural scenery; to which I had been indebted not only for much of the pleasure of my life, but quite recently for relief from one of my longest relapses into depression." But, as he went on to say, "Wordsworth would never have had any great effect on me, if he had merely placed before me beautiful pictures of natural scenery. . . . What made Wordsworth's poems a medicine for my state of mind, was that they expressed, not mere outward beauty, but states of feeling, and of thought coloured by feeling, under the excitement of beauty." [4] Here, as in "Wordsworth's Grave" and in the lines "To Edward Dowden," Wordsworth's peculiar source of solace for the Victorians—his ability to revive and revitalize the emotions through an appeal to nature and homely ways —is laid bare. "Wordsworth's Grave," then, is not only significant for what it reveals about Watson but also for what it tells us about his contemporaries; it is a fitting tribute from the late Victorians to Wordsworth whose poetry through the years had come to symbolize peace and rest—a homely, simple, rural life enhanced by nature, and hallowed by its "Presences."

Since Watson had found a kind reception for his "Ver Tenebrosum" in the pages of the conservative journal, the *National Review*, he sent the manuscript of "Wordsworth's Grave" to Alfred Austin and W. J. Courthope, the co-editors, who read it and were immediately impressed. Always proud of the fact that he had first published the famous elegy, Austin in his autobiography later told of his receipt of the poem, of his admiration for it, and of his rather thoughtless dispatch of a copy to Theodore Watts-Dunton who showed it to Swinburne. His expectations, of course, were sadly disappointed when he heard that neither Watts-Dunton nor Swinburne shared his views about the poem. Austin—and rightly so—attributed this hostile reaction to the fact that several lines in "Wordsworth's Grave"—especially "Lo, one with empty music floods the ear"—could be construed to refer either to Swinburne or to the poetry he favored. As Austin stated it, "I fancy their [Swinburne's and Watts-Dunton's] judgment was in some degree warped by a circumstance I had at first not noticed, that a stanza in "Wordsworth's Grave" might be interpreted by them as adverse to a style and school of Poetry that enjoyed their preference." [5]

Despite the reaction of Swinburne, "Wordsworth's Grave" first appeared in the pages of the *National Review* in September, 1887,[6] over three years after it was begun at Rydal. And although its reception at the time hardly prefigured the storm of approval it later evoked, friends such as Edward Dowden and James Ashcroft Noble were convinced of its greatness. Writing in 1888 about the young, still obscure poet, Noble said: "To the general reader Mr. Watson is largely unknown, but the future of his fame is certain, for his work is characterised by that grave sanity of thought and emotion, and that perfection of lucidly imaginative expression, which, amid all the chances and changes of literary fashion, constitute a valid claim to endurance in the memory of the world." [7] Noble's confident optimism was soon to be borne out, for there was still a large audience who shared the critic's notion of what constituted good poetry.

However, it was not until after the slender little volume in the blue paper boards entitled *Wordsworth's Grave and Other Poems* appeared in January, 1890, that fame came. For instance, in 1891, Edward Clodd, the author of "The Childhood of the World," and a man of intellectual stature and of widespread influence, was attracted to the volume which he showed to Thomas Hardy and Grant Allen, the critic, who both greeted the work with approval.[8] Under the auspices of Clodd, Watson soon met Grant Allen, and the way was prepared for the review which thrust the young poet into the limelight of the literary world.

II *Watson's Rise to Fame*

In a sonnet addressed to Clodd, Watson, recalling his long, bitter task "Of suitor at the world's reluctant ear," thanked his friend who

> earliest drew,
> On me obscure, that chivalrous regard,
> Ev'n his, who, knowing fame's first steep how hard,
> With generous lips no faltering clarion blew,
> Bidding men hearken to a lyre by few
> Heeded, . . . ("To Edward Clodd," II, 10)

And in his reference here to Grant Allen he rightly characterized that critic's kindness towards him and his review of *Wordsworth's Grave and Other Poems* which was, indeed, a trumpet which announced Watson to the world and bade all men hear. This review, modestly entitled "Note on a New Poet," appeared in the *Fortnightly* on August 1, 1891, and from this moment on Watson's fame soared to the heights. Overnight he found himself among the most popular poets of his day.

Grant Allen's uncanny ability to arouse interest in causes he chose to espouse was well-known in the 1890's, and Richard Le Gallienne recalled this quality some years later in his *Attitudes and Avowals* when he used the case of Watson to illustrate Allen's extraordinary gift as a publicist. "At one time," he observed, "Mr. Hutton seemed to edit *The Spectator* for the very proper purpose of announcing the truly momentous presence in our midst of the author of 'Wordsworth's Grave.' " But, despite efforts of his own and those of Ashcroft Noble to arouse interest in the poetry of the young poet, the issue of the *National Review* in which "Wordsworth's Grave" first appeared "passed virtually unnoticed" by the public and critics. With considerable irony directed toward Watson as well as Allen, Le Gallienne continued: "An unappreciated genius, Mr. Watson wandered unrecognised on the Yorkshire moors. Then Grant Allen took up his speaking trumpet, modestly enough, indeed, as he always did, and said: 'Let there be William Watson,' and there was William Watson. . . . Grant Allen had blown his trumpet, that 'coarse' trumpet of his, and England—including Lord Rosebery—heard." [9]

Without doubt, after Allen's review, Watson's little volume burst upon the English literary scene as if it were some sudden revelation of divine import. And Allen himself set the style when in the opening paragraphs of his review he compared his discovery of Watson's poetry to Keats's journey "thro' realms of gold." The moment of revelation occurred, Allen remarked, when Edward Clodd handed him the *Wordsworth's Grave* volume opened to the epigram on Shelley and Harriet Westbrook; one glimpse "revealed the gold. I looked up in surprise, and exclaimed at once, 'This is *not* minor poetry!' " [10] Continuing his rather pretentious allusion to Keats, Allen rapturously declared that "Whoever reads *Wordsworth's Grave* tearfully and prayerfully must feel at once that a new planet has swum into our ken; a planet which all watchers of our poetic skies will track with interest henceforth through its 'orbit in the spheres.' "

Despite the introduction which was written for effect, "Note on a New Poet" should not be taken lightly. As we shall see, a whole host of important men of literature (now far better known than Allen) responded to Watson's poetry with similar emotion. What Allen discovered of value and satisfaction in the *Wordsworth's Grave* volume were the very qualities which made Watson's widespread fame during the 1890's no hollow show. What Allen found was what a large, influential segment of English society, high and low, wanted and perhaps needed in poetry.

Allen's main point of emphasis was that "Mr. Watson's poetry is essentially of the Centre." And that Watson's work was traditional and in a sense conventional in subject matter and prosody was to Allen a means of suggesting the poet's uniqueness (a view which comes as rather a shock to us). Yet Allen was definitely making capital, so to speak, out of the fact that the most notable, or perhaps I should say notorious, poetry of the day had its *raison d'être* in flaunting its radicalism in the face of tradition. "Since Tennyson came and passed," Allen pointed out, "the tendency of English verse has been all towards obscurities, affectations, eccentricities. Here is a poet who moves in a circle round the common centre."

Counting on the majority of Victorians to rally to the banner of tradition and take up arms against the rather suspicious forces of the extreme, Allen based his whole effort to win fame for Watson on his solid traditionalism. *Wordsworth's Grave and Other Poems,* he assured his readers, "stands in the direct line of descent from the verse of the great early poets. In one word, it is orthodox— poetically, I mean, of course, not theologically orthodox. There is no heresy here, no hole-and-corner sectarianism." That Watson's poetry "belongs to the main stream," the critic noticed, is "its chief value, its secular merit, its lasting importance." Among other things, Allen praised the sanity, self-restraint, and good sense exhibited in Watson's work; and he claimed freshness and originality for the verse despite its close adherence to what he called the "beaten track." Although the poetry of *Wordsworth's Grave* was closest to the work of Landor and Arnold, Allen found that it had "a distinctive character of its own" and "a delicate refinement of detail in frieze and architrave" which gave "it an individual claim to attention among its flamboyant neighbors."

Perhaps overplaying the prevalence of unorthodox poetry and its often modest departures from the norm, Allen eloquently rose to the climax of his review in an overblown rhetorical effusion reminiscent of some of Watson's own prose passages: "There have been bards unintelligible, bards hysterical, bards nympholeptic, bards abstruse, bards spasmodic, bards inarticulate, and bards babbling or infantile; but for the most part there has been a want in our era of good sound common-sense married to good sound poetry, clear, terse, and polished. Mr. Watson has come in the nick of time to fill this aching void in our contemporary Helicon."

As one can see, Allen's review was a rather astute bit of propa-

ganda. Certainly it is difficult—especially in the light of Le Gallienne's remarks—not to look at the review as at least in part a
sheer piece of journalistic bravado written by a man who was
aware of and enjoyed revelling in his considerable powers as a
molder of public opinion. And, totally sincere or not, the "Note on
a New Poet" was carefully calculated to do exactly what it did ac-
complish: it won for Watson the status of a popular poet of
great promise in a traditional line of poetry suspiciously akin to
that of Wordsworth and of Alfred, Lord Tennyson, his phenom-
enally popular successor to the Poet Laureateship.

Wordsworth's Grave and Other Poems contained, in addition
to the title poem, the "Ver Tenebrosum" sonnets, a group of epigrams from the earlier volume, and several other poems composed at various times during the 1880's but never published,
such as "The Lute-Player," "World-Strangeness," "The Mock Self,"
"The Raven's Shadow," and a poem "On Landor's 'Hellenics'."
Until Allen's review appeared, the volume sold very poorly and
received only scattered reviews. But in addition to Allen's own
and Ashcroft Noble's efforts on behalf of Watson before the "Note"
appeared, Le Gallienne could have mentioned the names of several far more famous, important critics who had received prior to
Allen the *Wordsworth's Grave* volume with considerable favor.

Shortly after it appeared, Edward Dowden, in a letter to his
friend, Clement K. Shorter, the editor of the *Illustrated London
News*, wrote: "Should you see 'Wordsworth's Grave,' by W. Watson (Unwin's Cameo Series), I hope you will say a word to make
it known. It contains some most finely wrought verse." [11] Other
critics, too, found Watson's conscious artistry manifested in the finished and technically perfect verses. This characteristic and the
literary quality and, in particular, scholarly aura of most of the
poems in the volume attracted the attention of Yeats whose review "A Scholar Poet," which appeared in the *Providence Sunday Journal*, was one of the first and most significant commen-
taries. "In technique," wrote Yeats, Watson's poetry "is perfect. No
ill-chosen word ever jangles its serene and solemn meditation." [12]
So completely had Watson succeeded in suppressing his outbursts
of temper and the passionate elements in his nature in these
poems that Yeats—despite the "Ver Tenebrosum" sonnets—
thought of the volume as having been produced in "a quiet schol-

ar's room, where everything is well arranged, where no fierce emotion has ever come."

Perhaps overly anxious to see Watson as a kind of Paterian esthete, Yeats dwelt too much on the preciousness of Watson's style and on the scholarly artifice of his verse. Finding the volume full of poetry devoted to criticism, Yeats assumed that it had "sprung from the critical rather than the creative imagination." With a good deal of insight, Yeats concluded his review with the prediction that the "polished achievement" of the *Wordsworth's Grave* volume would hardly be duplicated "in the coming generation." "The coming struggle between capital and labor, of mysticism and science," he ominously surmised, "will more and more absorb or deafen into silence all such cloistered lives."

That *Wordsworth's Grave and Other Poems* was enjoying something of a vogue in America in 1891 is indicated by William Dean Howells in his review which appeared in his "Editor's Study" in *Harper's* of May, 1891. Apologizing to his readers for not having noticed Watson's poetry earlier, Howells observed that the volume "was published in London long enough ago last year to have become a cult in Boston. In its seventy-five pages," he continued, "there is very little that is not very good, . . ."[13]

Watson was always very appreciative of this American review and of one other written by Mrs. Louise Chandler Moulton for the *Boston Herald*. In a letter to Mrs. Moulton dated August 23, 1892, Watson expressed his gratitude to her, and berated himself for not having thanked Howells for his review:

Do you know—brute that I am—I have never written to another benefactor of mine, W. D. Howells, who like yourself wrote about me, most delightfully, in Harper's Magazine! But it is that cursed Atlantic that is really to blame. I cherish, however, a dream of crossing the pond some day myself, and if I should ever do so, there are two human beings whom I shall "make for" in Boston: one is Howells, innocent of the fate in store for him: the other is,—well you may guess. There's a threat for you![14]

Andrew Lang, Watson's opponent in the battle over the merits of Rider Haggard, reviewed *Wordsworth's Grave* in his feature "At the Sign of the Ship" in *Longman's Magazine* in November, 1891; and—still not knowing that Watson was "The Writer of 'The

Fall of Fiction'"—he gave the work a fair, accurate appraisal. Complaining about all the worthless volumes of poetry issuing from the press, Lang singled out *Wordsworth's Grave* as being "so different from these." Although he declared that "Mr. Watson's poetry, indeed, is of the second rank," he was otherwise in substantial agreement with most other critics when he remarked that the volume "is purely literary; it contains not much but criticism in verse: but then the verse is so excellent that we may call it finished and almost perfect." [15] Unable to rank Watson "with original poets, still less with great poets," Lang, nevertheless, praised Watson's "poetic sympathies," his "mastery of his instrument," and the poet's "delicacy, and grace, and heart."

Besides Thomas Hardy's admiration for *Wordsworth's Grave*, A. E. Housman, who always spoke well of Watson, once wrote that the little volume was "one of the precious things of English literature." [16] But there can be little doubt that of all the commendations Watson's *Wordsworth's Grave and Other Poems* received, the brief letter from Tennyson pleased the author most. Written from Farringford on December 20, 1891, the letter from the aged laureate contained these words: "I thank you; for to me who receive every morning, or all but every morning, in print or in MSS, verses, verses, verses, the voice of a poet and a patriot must all the more be grateful." [17]

Since Allen's "Note on a New Poet" appeared in August, 1891, attention in the form of reviews, letters, and sales was showered at last on the Yorkshire poet who now moved to London, received the dying laureate's blessing, and prepared to enter upon that momentous year of fame which could—but for a strange and malicious quirk of fate—have seen his accession in triumph to the chair of Tennyson.

III *The Fateful Year*

As the new year dawned, the name of William Watson was a frequent one on the lips of literary critics and devotees of poetry; and by March it was not unusual to see in print remarks such as E. K. Chambers' to the effect that Watson was generally recognized "as the most promising of our younger poets." [18] Just why Watson suddenly emerged from obscurity at the beginning of the last Victorian decade can never be certainly known. But I suspect it was due primarily to the fact that by 1891 the great traditional poets of the nineteenth century had, like Arnold, recently died, or, like Tennyson, withdrawn into deep seclusion; yet the poetry they wrote was still to many the only kind of poetry they knew and could accept. And as I have indicated before, the poetic idiom of the Miltonic tradition seemed to have a soothing, sustaining effect which the poetry of the esthetes and radical versifiers did not possess. Strange though it seems to us, many by 1891 had already had enough of Wilde (and those of similar tastes) even though they had to wait until 1895 to crush him. Consequently, Watson's "poetry of the Centre" was exactly what could be expected to satisfy a large audience at this particular time; and I imagine that a number of influential publishers and critics—masters at gauging the temper of the reading public—recognized this fact. Although there is no tangible evidence, Watson's sudden rise to fame and the key roles played in it by literary men of the day—such as Clodd, Hutton, Meredith Townsend, Allen, Clement Shorter, Walter Besant, Coulson Kernahan, Dowden, Austin, Noble, and others—suggest more than a mere disinterested, unorganized effort to aid a friend. Could it have been that, even before the death of Tennyson, the battle to name his successor had begun? That powerful forces on the London literary scene had already chosen their candidates and had thus early made their first moves? Watson's fame was so closely tied up with the longest, most bitterly fought laureateship battle in literary annals that it is difficult not to see him as the front for a group of powerful literary figures who wanted the privilege of having enthroned the next laureate.

Anyone surveying the literary scene in England about 1890 could not help but see that Tennyson's death (which certainly was imminent) would create a need for a traditional poet trained in the Miltonic poetic idiom and dedicated to the sentiments and thematic preoccupations of the great Victorians; and the shocking, uneasy effect which much poetry since Swinburne had made on the public only added to the urgency of this demand. And even if a majority of the nation had been willing to see a Swinburne or a Wilde drape himself in the mantel of the beloved Tennyson, would Victoria approve? After all the laureate was her choice. To be sure the queen would not have been amused if her

prime minister had dared to suggest a poet other than a Tennysonian—and astute critics knew this. Watson's poetry and his poetic creed were clearly appropriate. His best known poem,
"Wordsworth's Grave," was beyond reproach. All that was needed
to launch him on the road to the laureateship was not only a vigorous campaign to advertise his virtues to the public but a volume or two more of poetry. Action to fulfill these two require-
ments was the work of 1892.

The task of advertising Watson's poetical merits had begun long
before Allen's review marked the beginning of what appears to be
a concerted effort. And that the theme of earlier commentators
became the keynote of the poet's sympathetic critics is indicated
by comparing "Note on a New Poet" with Richard Holt Hutton's
review of 1890, "Mr. Watson's Poems." Hutton's approach was to
sell Watson's fine craftsmanship, his conservative tastes, and his
traditionalism by juxtaposing them with the attributes of his dis-
reputable contemporaries. Making a direct appeal to the earnest,
respectable Victorian reader of poetry, Hutton declared that Watson "has something to say which is worth saying. He is very much
in earnest, but he is neither dull, nor denunciatory, nor despond-
ent." [19] Then he proceeded to make the usual comparison: "Many
of our modern poetmasters run riot in the direction of elaborate
metrical experiments after the antique. Or else, while making a
brave parade of antinomianism they only convey an impression
of their intense weariness of spirit. But here is a young singer who
is wholesomely free from the maladie du siècle, a deep lover of
the country, a fervent patriot, and a genuine Wordsworthian to
boot."

Once the correct critical approach to Watson was established,
all that was needed was more poetry; and Watson was apparently
equal to the task. By January, 1892, publishers and journals were
clamoring for his work; and the poet soon prepared an edition of
old and new poems which Macmillan published in February entitled simply *Poems*. Composed of the entire contents of the second edition of *Wordsworth's Grave* and a number of pieces which
had recently been published in various journals, it also included
Watson's elegy on Matthew Arnold, "In Laleham Churchyard."
Employing the stanzaic form Burns used so effectively in the
"Epistle to J. Lapraik," Watson clearly had in mind Wordsworth's

threnody, "At the Grave of Burns," when he wrote his poem in August, 1890. And perhaps Wordsworth's celebration of the Scotsman's humble life close to the soil, his thwarted aspirations, and his simple but heartfelt verses predisposed Watson to view Matthew Arnold's cultivated, urbane, scholarly manner with a somewhat jaundiced eye. With one eye on Wordsworth's "At the Grave of Burns" and with the other on his own "Wordsworth's Grave," Watson composed his threnody on Arnold. Consequently one is inclined to feel that with Burns and Wordsworth on the opposite side, the scales were loaded against Arnold from the commencing " 'Twas" to the concluding "yet." Throughout the entire poem an implied comparison between Arnold and Wordsworth exists. Rotha, the stream by which Wordsworth sleeps, with its mountain setting and its turbulent, uneasy flow, is juxtaposed with the "unruffled tide" and plain setting of the Thames by which Arnold lies buried. And the presence of the warm, emotionally responsive, rather naïve poet eulogized in "Wordsworth's Grave" shines through the gloom of Watson's rather sedate, tepid portrait of Arnold. Always sentimentally inclined to compare the poet who sang "of lowly weal and dole" to the detriment of the poet who "shunned the common stain and smutch," Watson's Arnold who stands aloof

> From soilure of ignoble touch
> Too grandly free,
> Too loftily secure in such
> Cold purity,

comes off rather badly when compared with Watson's Wordsworth whose humble lays "from the soul leapt instant to the soul."

Lacking emotional spontaneity, the Arnold who now lay in Laleham Churchyard had carried his pose of disinterestedness too far. Caring only to preserve "from chance control/ The fortress of his 'stablisht soul," he, proudly aloof, looked with disdain upon the common lot of simple men. Unlike the "impassioned quietude" which characterized Wordsworth's mind and art, Arnold's genius was typified by "Its strength, its grace,/ Its lucid gleam, its sober pride,/ Its tranquil pace." Thus, as the elegy moves through its melancholy verses, and its explicit and implicit comparisons,

to its close, the reader is prepared for the final contrast between
Arnold, who with unruffled ease seemed to carry all before him,
and Burns, who vainly struggled against overwhelming odds:

> Great is the facile conqueror;
> Yet haply he, who, wounded sore,
> Breathless, unhorsed, all covered o'er
>   With blood and sweat,
> Sinks foiled, but fighting evermore,—
>   Is greater yet.

Needless to say, this rather damning conclusion has not only
shocked but puzzled readers ever since it first appeared in the
pages of the *Spectator* on August 30, 1890. For it was apparent
even then that Watson personally as well as poetically was closer
to Arnold than he was to Wordsworth. To be sure, "The deep,
authentic mountain-thrill/ Ne'er shook" Arnold's page, but neither
did it enliven the verses of Watson. Yeats in "A Scholar Poet" had
been quick to see that Watson belonged with writers like Matthew Arnold "who have nothing extravagant, exuberant, mystical"
to say; who are not so much "inspired" as they are "accom-
plished." Unhesitatingly, Yeats had placed Watson "Among the
younger men who follow the Matthew Arnold tradition." [20] And
later P. G. L. Webb went further when he pointed out that "In
choice of subject and vein of thought Mr. Watson is more nearly
akin to Arnold than to any other English poet." [21] In other words,
as Charles Hunter Ross expressed it, "both have the note—a discontent with present conditions, a high seriousness of style, an instinct for higher thinking and living." [22] Concerned specifically
with Watson's response to Arnold in the elegy, Edward A. Valentine was puzzled by the fact that Watson generously acknowl-
edged Wordsworth's influence in "Wordsworth's Grave" but
failed "to register an equal debt to Matthew Arnold." After all,
the critic remarked, "It is really through Arnold that he ap-
proaches nature's shrine; it is with not a little of that poet's scholarly constraint and lack of joyousness he views the panorama of
earth, sea and sky." [23]

Whatever the motive might have been which led Watson to conclude "In Laleham Churchyard" with such an unfavorable com-

ment, it was probably not a capricious one. Almost certainly those lines in "Wordsworth's Grave" "And some parade a conscious naturalness,/ The scholar's not the child's simplicity" refer to Arnold and imply the same criticism made explicit in the later elegy: Arnold was too intellectual, too polished and urbane to suit Watson. Seeing in Arnold the same tendencies toward pessimism, agnosticism, and world-weariness which plagued his own soul, Watson envied the outward self-possession, the apparent ease with which Arnold suppressed his deep and melancholy fears, rose superior, and stood imperturbably aloof above all his great misgivings. Watson of humble background, scanty formal education, and few pretensions to the grace and style or to the intellectual prowess of the cultured élite, could not help but envy an Arnold who appeared to the struggling young poet to be a "facile conqueror."

Poems was well received by reviewers and public alike, and during the spring months Watson was steadily supplying important journals such as the *Spectator,* the *Speaker,* and the *Illustrated London News* with essays[24] and with poems like "The Things That Are More Excellent" which proved very popular. Besides these many short poems, Watson had been working during the winter of 1891–92 on his first long philosophical poem which was to appear in the *Lachrymae Musarum* volume as "The Dream of Man." Working steadily through most of the summer of 1892, Watson found the demands of his publishers and the strain of nursing an ill, aged mother almost more than he could bear; but no let-up was in sight. His increasing irritability, nervous frustration, chronic appendicitis, and psychosomatic illnesses during the late summer and early autumn of 1892 are evidenced in his letters of this period and in the various reports of him in reminiscences and in other documents of his acquaintances. For instance, the letters which he exchanged with Louise Chandler Moulton from late July through early October clearly indicate Watson's unhappy state of mind.

Mrs. Moulton often journeyed to England where she settled in London for considerable periods of time which she spent entertaining her "troops of friends." Her admiration for Watson's poetry naturally led her to seek him out during the sojourn of 1892. Consequently, it was not long before Watson heard that his kind critic would like to see him at one of her "at homes" which she regularly held on Thursday afternoons at 23 Weymouth Street, Portland Place. In his first letter to her written from his residence at Yokohoma, Crown Hill, Upper Norwood, and dated July 24[?], 1892, Watson wrote that he would very much like to visit her, but "I am at present kept at home by a slight illness, & living at an inconvenient distance from the railway I am seldom able to get into town at all." [25] Watson's ensuing letters, like the initial one, are usually in the nature of an apology. Although he did succeed in attending the American lady's "at homes," he often found that "circumstances made it quite impossible" for him to get into town. As August wore on and the time for Mrs. Moulton's departure drew near, Watson's reasons for his infrequent attendance upon her grew more explicit. In his letter of August 23 he apologized for not seeing her on the previous Wednesday. It was not the bad weather, he explained, "but domestic matters which I have no excuse for boring you with a recital of, [which] made it quite impossible for me to get into town that day." Then Watson went on to say that, if he did not see her on the following Thursday, she was to set down his

non-appearance to insuperable impediments, for none other shall be permitted to prevent me. As a matter of fact my personal responsibilities are very heavy, and I am oppressed with perhaps more work than one man ought to have to do, so that the difficulty of getting into town from here (where my distance from rail is considerable) is very great, owing to the time consumed in going and coming. Hence I am obliged to forfeit almost all the social opportunities placed within my reach, to my great misfortune.

Watson's next letter, dated September 16, is interesting because he speaks openly about his rather trying domestic situation and details some of his professional preoccupations:

You have a deal to forgive, in my long silence—but I have only been *apparently* neglectful, not really so. My mother has been very ill, again and again—my cottage dominated by a nurse, dread despot! (rather good-looking—the one redeeming circumstance: yet I didn't flirt with her, sure as I'm a rhymer!) And all this while I have been tremendously busy, boiling the pot, &c. &c. Macmillan and Co will print next month a tiny new vol. of mine—"The Dream of Man," & other poems. It has a dedication "To London my hostess" & an epilogue, "To England my mother." The latter I print in the *Spectator*—next Saturday, I believe.

In his last letter to Mrs. Moulton before her departure for America, written on October 3 from his new residence at St. Malo, Clifton Terrace, Southend-on-Sea, Watson referred to his recent fit of wanderlust: "We have been feeling so unsettled—and indeed haven't a proper sense of fixity yet. I inherit a wandering instinct from my father, who was never happy under one roof more than about a year: and I give the Post-Office as much trouble as I can."

During his stay at Southend, Watson wrote one of his rare comic poems, *The Eloping Angels;* and from the way in which he referred to it in this letter, one can see his Victorian uneasiness at spending time in so questionable a manner: "I have been guilty of a longish poem since I came here, called 'the Eloping Angels: a caprice.' It is in a light vein, partly. I have not been much afflicted lately with thoughts that do often lie too deep for tears—hence my excursion into levity. But I threaten to be tremendously serious next time."

Speaking rather desperately about his secluded state, Watson continued: "I have not been once in town since I left Norwood, and begin to forget how people speak or dress or otherwise deport themselves in London. This seems a suitable place for growing a beard, or embarking on any other speculative enterprise requiring seclusion from the madding crowd. The proximity of the Kernahans was necessary to prevent me from lapsing into utter savagery in these desert wilds."

On October 6, three days after Watson penned his letter to Mrs. Moulton, his ills and frustrations were suddenly thrust into the background when the news reached him of Tennyson's death at Aldworth. An urgent telegram from the editor of the *Illustrated London News* commissioned Watson to write a short poem eulogizing the dead laureate. Watson, who lost no time responding to the task, closeted himself, according to his brother Robinson, for fifty consecutive hours after which he emerged with the finest of all the elegies on Tennyson, "Lachrymae Musarum." According to Coulson Kernahan, who was with him at the time, Watson composed and perfected the entire poem in his head before he sat

down and wrote out the completed poem—another instance of
the poet's amazing memory.[26] The elegy appeared in the *Illustrated London News* on October 15, three days after Watson attended Tennyson's funeral in Westminster Abbey as an honorary
pallbearer.

Watson's memory also served him in another way in "Lachrymae Musarum." Its solemn, stately verse; its rich often latinate
diction; and its melodius vowel sounds—especially the double
"o's" and "u's"—echo Tennyson's fine "Ode on the Death of the
Duke of Wellington." That Watson had the gift of catching the
authentic note of the poet whom he was eulogizing and thereby of
heightening the effect is shown in the very Tennysonian opening
stanza of the elegy:

> Lo, like another's, lies the laurelled head:
> The life that seemed a perfect song is o'er:
> Carry the last great bard to his last bed.
> Land that he loved, thy noblest voice is mute.
> Land that he loved, that loved him! nevermore
> Meadow of thine, smooth lawn or wild sea-shore,
> Gardens of odorous bloom and tremulous fruit,
> Or woodlands old, like Druid couches spread,
> The master's feet shall tread.
> Death's little rift hath rent the faultless lute:
> The singer of undying songs is dead. (I, 3)

Again, the central stanzas of the poem which describe Tennyson's apotheosis illustrate the effect of Watson's memory on his
poetry when he unconsciously echoed Shelley's "Adonais" in the
following verses:

> Nay, he returns to regions whence he came.
> Him doth the spirit divine
> Of universal loveliness reclaim.
> All nature is his shrine.
> Seek him henceforward in the wind and sea,
> In earth's and air's emotion or repose,
> In every star's august serenity,
> And in the rapture of the flaming rose.
> There seek him if ye would not seek in vain,
> There, in the rhythm and music of the Whole. (I, 5)

In fact, the whole concluding portion of "Adonais" from Stanza
XXXVIII onward must have been ringing in Watson's ears when
he wrote the central stanzas of "Lachrymae Musarum"; for not only
is the doctrine of immortality identical with the kind of neo-
Platonic pantheism Shelley employed, but the wording and images are similar.[27] Thus again Watson vitalized the effect of his
stanzas by a kind of overtone effect, or Shelleyan aura, obtained by
recalling to the reader's mind the lovely musical verses in which
Shelley celebrated the immortality of Keats.

If Wordsworth was Watson's "spiritual king," Tennyson was his
great image of the public bard—the perfect embodiment of the
poet laureateship; and this pose was certainly the main source of
Watson's admiration. None of the great poet-prophets of the past
stood so austerely magnificent before his mind as did Tennyson.
This "last great bard," his enviable image in the public eye, was
everything that Watson someday longed to be. Throughout the
"Lachrymae," Watson was conscious of Tennyson as the latest of
the sovereign line of bards. Alluding to his visit with Tennyson
some years before, Watson cherished the notion that, by grasping
the great poet's hand, he had touched through him

> . . . the hand
> Of every hero of thy race divine,
> Ev'n to the sire of all the laurelled line,
> The sightless wanderer on the Ionian strand.

This same note was struck earlier in his sonnet "To Lord Tennyson" when Watson celebrated him as

> Heir of the riches of the whole world's rhyme,
> Dow'r'd with the Doric grace, the Mantuan mien,
> With Arno's depth and Avon's golden sheen;
> Singer to whom the singing ages climb,
> Convergent. (*Poems* [London, 1892], p. 41)

That Watson thought of himself as a poet of this great bardic tradition and aspired himself to play a role in perpetuating it is indicated by the closing lines of the sonnet:

> —if the youngest of the choir
> May snatch a flying splendour from your name

Making his page illustrious, and aspire
For one rich moment your regard to claim,
Suffer him at your feet to lay his lyre
And touch the skirts and fringes of your fame.

Among the important poems in the *Lachrymae Musarum* volume is Watson's chief poetic tribute to Shelley written on the occasion of the one-hundredth anniversary of the poet's birth which occurred on August 4, 1892. Entitled simply "Shelley's Centenary," the poem is another interesting example of Watson's ability to evoke the spirit of his subject by weaving into its texture words and allusions which recall to our minds the poet's authentic voice. In evoking Shelley's love for the atmospheric beauty of light, air, cloud, and water, Watson incorporated phrases from "The Cloud," "Ode to the West Wind," "Epipsychidion," "Prometheus Unbound," and "Lines Written Among the Euganean Hills." [28]

With his usual relish for cataloguing the poets of the past and for characterizing their essential qualities, Watson commenced the poem with a comparison and contrast between Byron, Shelley, and Keats. Employing once more the "Burns stanza," he highlighted Shelley's essential nature by juxtaposing it with attributes of his famous contemporaries:

Alike remote from Byron's scorn,
And Keats's magic as of morn
Bursting for ever newly-born
        On forests old,
To wake a hoary world forlorn
        With touch of gold,

Shelley, the cloud-begot, who grew
Nourished on air and sun and dew,
Into that Essence whence he drew
        His life and lyre
Was fittingly resolved anew
        Through wave and fire. (I, 53)

Successfully evoking the ethereality of Shelley and his impatience of material limitations, Watson, nevertheless, found this preoccupation with the visionary and other-worldly a serious flaw. Shel-

ley's admirable but naïve desire to regenerate the will of man and
to build a divine world in a day was vain, in Watson's opinion, and
indicated a lack of knowledge about the true nature of the world.
As his Dr. Johnson once said: "No, Sir; Mr. Shelley can talk flu-
ently enough about man, but men he seemed not to have encountered." [29] To be sure, Shelley's "wild assault upon the Past,"
his spirit of revolt, was, according to Watson, equally as vain as
were his idealistic notions about man's future. But even though
Watson's late nineteenth-century world was molded "In other
shapes than he forecast,"

> . . . what shall last
> Is that pure strain,
>
> Which seems the wandering voices blent
> Of every virgin element,—
> A sound from ocean caverns sent,—
> An airy call
> From the pavilioned firmament
> O'erdoming all.
>
> And in this world of worldlings, where
> Souls rust in apathy, and ne'er
> A great emotion shakes the air,
> And life flags tame,
> And rare is noble impulse, rare
> The impassioned aim,
>
> 'Tis no mean fortune to have heard
> A singer who, if errors blurred
> His sight, had yet a spirit stirred
> By vast desire,
> And ardour fledging the swift word
> With plumes of fire. (I, 55)

Certainly Shelley's prophetic gift suggested in these lines and his
ability to impart to others his vision of higher things were recognized and valued by Watson. In his essay on "Shelley as Poet,"
Watson singled out as Shelley's "grand characteristic" his "inspired
manner—the tone, the accent, the air of being but a medium of
communication, the conducting channel between his hearers and

some more elemental influence, which the primitive imagination personified as the Muse." In one of his better moments as a critic, Watson concluded: "What Shelley does give, as no other poet can, is a heightened and rapturous sense of the splendours and wonder of existence." [30]

Lachrymae Musarum and Other Poems was a resounding success and did much to establish Watson as a contender for the laureateship during the initial stages of the long battle. Graham R. Tomson's review for the *Academy* welcomed the new volume "as a mountain breeze across the 'sick leagues' of redundance and unrestrained expression, through which the jaded student of modern verse must labour, day in day out." [31] And the reviewer for the *Spectator* (probably Richard Holt Hutton) responded to the book exactly as one might have predicted. Putting Watson forward as a poet of the first rank, the critic was of the opinion that "The poem on Tennyson's death is alone sufficient to make a great name."

With more than a hint that Watson was preeminently qualified for the laureateship, the *Spectator's* spokesman, continuing his remarks about the title poem, asserted that "A man who can give the highest distinction to the expression of every cultivated man's feeling, is more likely to become a great poet than the man who can only give similar expression to thoughts which have sprung up in his own mind with all the vigour of original conception and all the notes of a fastidious discrimination." Because of its disturbing picture of man's destiny and its unorthodox view of God, the reviewer found "The Dream of Man" "an ambitious failure" and attempted to explain it away as a rare but understandable error in judgment on the poet's part. Watson's advisers no doubt deplored this rather depressing departure from orthodoxy at this time as much as they objected to his violent prose attacks on the popular novelists and scholars of the day.

Despite some reservations on the part of various critics, "Lachrymae Musarum" was clearly recognized by all to be the best of the elegies written at this time on the death of Tennyson—a clearcut victory for Watson which enabled his supporters to bring pressure to bear on Gladstone to award the poet a Civil List Pension. And although Gladstone, who did admire Watson's poetry when it was brought to his attention, was unable to give Watson the pension, he did award his a £200 gift from the Royal Bounty Fund on November 17.³² This action, of course, was immediately interpreted by press and public as a mark of special favor on the part of the prime minister. One can imagine how much strain this attention added to Watson's already overburdened mind. Not only fame and fortune were now resting on his abilities to produce but also the prize he most coveted, the laureateship.

On October 22, *Lyric Love*, his edition of great love poems of the language, had appeared in the Golden Treasury Series; and, by November, Watson was preparing *The Eloping Angels* and *Excursions in Criticism* for publication by Elkin Mathews and John Lane, as well as a new edition of his collected poems for Macmillan. As the fateful year drew to a close, pressure on the rapidly rising poet increased proportionately. Nervousness, insomnia, irritability, and stomach ailments became a steady part of Watson's hectic life. Outbursts of temper which grew more frequent and uncontrolled finally became public spectacles. Late in November, for instance, a dispute with Macmillan over payment for editing *Lyric Love* led the poet to denounce his publisher in a series of rather astonishing tirades delivered in the presence of a number of distinguished persons first in the smoking room of the Devonshire Club and later in such places as the drawing room of Lady Lyalt's town house and as the precincts of the National Liberal Club.³³ As the winter drew on, Watson evidently resorted to heavy drinking to calm his nerves and to chloral to induce sleep.³⁴

Then on Wednesday, December 7, he journeyed to Windsor where he called on A. C. Benson apparently in the hope that the Eton don would gain him an audience with his father, the Archbishop of Canterbury. Laboring under the delusion that he had some astounding revelation to make concerning corruption "in high places," Watson also sent three strange, incoherent cables to his brother James in New York while he continued to communicate with Benson who, thoroughly alarmed by his strange talk, wrote to Edmund Gosse in London requesting that he notify Watson's family that the poet was very ill. Finally on Sunday, December 11, the inevitable occurred in a most unfortunate and unexpected manner. To allay his restlessness and sense of anxiety, Watson insisted on taking a stroll with his brother Robinson, who had earlier in the day arrived to care for him. On coming to the long walk leading to Windsor Castle, the pair met a royal coach carrying the Duke of Edinburgh and his family.[35] Suddenly Watson darted out into the path of the oncoming vehicle, seized the reins, and attempted to stop the horses and enter the carriage. Police were immediately summoned, the violently insane poet was arrested on the spot, and rushed off to jail. At the hearing on Monday morning, he had still not regained his mental balance and raved incoherently. Needless to say, Watson's words on this occasion were elaborately reported in the newspapers that evening and on the following day in England and America. The New York *Times*, for instance, gave one of the milder, more restrained accounts when it reported that Watson, during the hearing "said that Milton was Sampson reincarnated, and that he himself was reincarnated Milton. He said that during the night messages flashed like lightning through his room; that Dalilah had been reincarnated to tempt him, but he had kept himself pure. He made other similarly incoherent statements. Dr. Ellison testified that the poet was insane, and he was accordingly sent to an asylum."[36] The staid London *Times*, which gave but a brief paragraph to the incident on Tuesday, December 13, reported more briefly still the final word on Wednesday, December 14: "Mr. William Watson, the poet, was removed yesterday to the Stone Lunatic Asylum, near Aylesbury."[37]

Watson's mental breakdown came as an appalling shock to his recently won public on both sides of the Atlantic; but, of course, it did not come so unexpectedly to his family and to close friends who no doubt noticed the increasing signs of mania and who recalled his illness of 1880. One of the first reports on Watson's progress after his illness pointed out that "The mental aberration, which came to a crisis at Windsor, had not been unheralded, and did not take those who have seen much of Mr. Watson recently greatly by surprise."[38]

Naturally, speculation as to the cause of the poet's illness ran rife in literary circles and often was reported in the papers. James Ashcroft Noble in his personal reminiscence of Watson written shortly after the breakdown commented on the widespread belief that the mental illness was "due to the excitement born of sudden success after long years spent in apparently vain attempts to catch the ear of the reading public," and tacitly agreed. Then he went on to say that no one knew better than he "how weary and disheartening seemed that time of waiting to one who, though he had his period of depression and dubitation, never lost consciousness of his real power." [39]

Another old and close friend, Charles A. Berry, was likewise of the opinion that Watson's long years of unrewarded labor and his sudden rise to fame brought on the crisis. In a letter to the editor of the *British Weekly* he wrote that he could not "wonder that a mind such as his [Watson's] should suffer temporary derangement, especially considering the long discipline and the fluctuations of literary emotion through which he has passed. . . . There is," he continued, "infinite pathos in the sight of a man who has borne suffering with fortitude, and unappreciation with calm patience, bending and almost breaking under the tardy yet generous recognition of his grateful fellow-countrymen." [40]

Indeed, fame had come at last to William Watson in his thirty-fourth year. But the singer who had risen to heal and arm and plenish and sustain could not, ironically, save himself. The year that was kindled with the bright sparks of fame had ended in a blaze of notoriety.

CHAPTER 5

Vita Nuova

> I too have come through wintry terrors,—yea,
> Through tempest and through cataclysm of soul
> Have come, and am delivered.
> —William Watson, "Vita Nuova"

DESPITE the seriousness of his illness and the length of his convalescence, Watson's recently won fame did not diminish. In fact, the nature and sensational onset of the malady enhanced his vogue and increased the sales of his works. And although his recovery was painfully slow, extending as it did over the entire year of 1893, volumes prepared prior to his illness appeared in the spring and effectually kept his name before the public. Early in the new year Macmillan brought out a new collected edition of the poetry entitled *The Poems of William Watson* which contained the complete contents of *Poems, Lachrymae Musarum and Other Poems, The Prince's Quest and Other Poems,* and fifty epigrams.

Then in March The Bodley Head published *The Eloping Angels: a Caprice* and a collection of Watson's prose, *Excursions in Criticism.* Of this group of works, only *The Eloping Angels* was entirely new. It and "The Dream of Man" reflect Watson's reading of Goethe's *Faust* and represent a humorous and a serious treatment of the theme of aspiration and striving. Watson, like Goethe's Faustian God, believed that struggle and strife in themselves were essential to man's happiness and well-being. Thus in "The Dream of Man," Watson, criticizing modern man's haughty confidence in his power to ultimately control the entire universe and conquer all ills, envisioned man as at last overcoming his greatest foe, Death, only to find that, in pushing aside the last obstacle, he had destroyed the source of happiness. In contrast to this approach to the subject is the comic irony with which the poet surrounds the same theme in *The Eloping Angels*. Despite the tasteful design and format of the three issues of the poem's first edition, "the caprice" was not well received by the critics. And although a second edition appeared in 1894, it became known as perhaps Watson's most dismal failure.

In April, Watson's lyric which celebrated a momentary revival of his spirits, "Vita Nuova," appeared in the *Spectator*.[1] Spring had come and with it a resurgence of vital spirits within the convalescent poet. In an exuberant second stanza reminiscent of similar passages in Wordsworth's *Prelude*, Watson exclaimed his joyous feelings of renewal:

> O ancient streams, O far-descended woods
> Full of the fluttering of melodious souls;
> O hills and valleys that adorn yourselves
> In solemn jubilation; winds and clouds,
> Ocean and land in stormy nuptials clasped,
> And all exuberant creatures that acclaim
> The Earth's divine renewal: lo, I too
> With yours would mingle somewhat of glad song. (I, 105)

But Watson's "thankful tears," which in "Vita Nuova" he dedicated

> To whatsoever Power beneficent,
> Veiled though his countenance, undivulged his thought,
> Hath led me from the haunted darkness forth
> Into the gracious air and vernal morn, (I, 106)

were unfortunately a bit premature. For the poet relapsed into long months of silence, loneliness, and depression from which he only began to emerge fully toward the end of the year. Nevertheless, the poem served to reassure his public of the poet's return to life, as an item in the April issue of the *Bookman* makes clear: "Mr. William Watson has returned from Switzerland, and has joined his mother at Southend. All his admirers will be glad to hear that Mr. Watson has completely recovered, and that so long as he keeps from overwork or undue excitement there is, we are assured, no danger of a return of his malady." [2]

I Odes and Other Poems

Actually Watson's complete recovery after a long, painful convalescence was signaled by the publication of his short story, "The Two Dorothys," in March, 1894,[3] and *Odes and Other Poems* on November 30, 1894. Containing thirty-six short pieces written largely since his breakdown, the volume marked no radical departure in theme or mode from the earlier works. If anything, the most notable poems indicate an increased preoccupation on the part of Watson with themes which deal with a decline in the taste and moral stamina of English society. Several poems contrast the strength and ethical grandeur of the past with the feebleness and moral degeneracy of the present. That Watson's attitude toward the human condition was becoming steadily more pessimistic is indicated by the prominence given the theme of war in the volume. Always unusually sensitive to situations and conditions which might lead to outbreaks of violence, Watson found ample cause for alarm in the growing antagonisms arising between the great nations of Europe during the feverish era of imperialistic expansion and exploitation. Furthermore, the early theme of "The high enigmas" [4] reasserts itself in *Odes and Other Poems* with considerable force. Always a source of uneasiness and depression, Watson's inability to find intellectually convincing answers to the riddles of life and death plagued him now more than ever. But even though the new volume revealed that a new lease on life had only increased his obsession with the decadent tendencies of his age, Watson's faith in the high mission of poetry in an iron age had not been shaken. The poet's commitment to the world in which he lived, his duty to guide and inspirit as well as to chastise, is reasserted with considerable vigor in the volume.

In a sonnet entitled, "Christmas Day," Watson continued his indictment of the increasingly shallow, materialistic tendencies of the England of the 1890's. His society's callous disregard of the spiritual significance of "Christ's natal day" was to Watson symbolic of the nation's sure decline. The sombre, melancholy state of decadence so clearly expressed in the sestet is hardly relieved by the Shelleyan prophecy of a regenerate world:

[100]

Fated among time's fallen leaves to stray,
We breathe an air that savours of the tomb,
Heavy with dissolution and decay;
Waiting till some new world-emotion rise,
And with the shattering might of the simoom
Sweep clean this dying Past that never dies. (II, 4)

Watson's attitude toward the 1890's is further indicated in this volume in a sonnet later entitled "Barren Levity" in which the poet's extreme aversion to the cynically aloof pose and to the irreverent humor of *fin-de-siècle* wits such as Oscar Wilde is clearly indicated. Watson, sharing for the moment the vantage point of the grave with "the immortal servants of mankind," mourned with them modern

. . . Man's barren levity of mind,
The ear to no grave harmonies inclined,
The witless thirst for false wit's worthless lees,
The laugh mistimed in tragic presences,
The eye to all majestic meanings blind. (II, 5)

The disturbing events on the international scene during the 1890's are reflected in the sonnet, "Peace and War," in which Watson presented man's condition as analogous to that of the cruel, amoral sea which is alternately calm and tempestuous: "So, betwixt Peace and War, man's life is cast"; and, even though man forever dreams "of perfect Peace at last," the sombre realist could only conclude that "The inconstant, moody ocean shall as soon,/ At the cold dictates of the bloodless moon,/ Swear an eternity of halcyon sleep" (II, 6).

In addition to this rather morbid sonnet, Watson's response to the increasingly explosive situations rapidly developing around the world is most strikingly expressed in "The World in Armour," his series of three sonnets. Aware of the ancient enmities and long-standing rivalries which lurked behind the complexities of European power politics, Watson in his second sonnet reminded his readers of the remnants of the Black Plague which lurked about "Till the dread Fire, one roaring wave of fate,/ Rose, and swept clean his last retreat and hold." Ominously he pointed to the "Dregs of full many an ancient Plague and dire,/ Old wrongs, old lies of ages blind and cruel," which existed in the Europe of his day. Prophetically, he brought the poem to a climax with the question: "What if alone the world-war's world-wide fire/ Can purge the ambushed pestilence away?" (II, 48).

In the final sonnet, with unerring accuracy and far more perspicacity than most of his contemporaries, the poet beheld

> The Europe of the present, as she stands,
> Powerless from terror of her own vast power,
> 'Neath novel stars, beside a brink unknown;
> And round her the sad Kings, with sleepless hands,
> Piling the fagots, hour by doomful hour. (II, 49)

Watson's inability to be at ease in the 1890's was also due in part to a kind of malady which he shared with many of his post-Darwinian countrymen. Earlier in "An Epistle" (which first appeared in *Poems*) Watson had voiced a persistent complaint of his age when he wrote:

> For still the ancient riddles mar
> Our joy in man, in leaf, in star.
> The Whence and Whither give no rest,
> The Wherefore is a hopeless quest. (I, 163)

And in *Odes and Other Poems,* the poet's preoccupation with this theme is evident in two sonnets in particular. "Not mine your mystic creed; not mine, in prayer/ And worship, at the ensanguined Cross to kneel," he wrote in his poem "To Aubrey De Vere":

> But when I mark your faith how pure and fair,
> How based on love, on passion for man's weal,
> My mind, half envying what it cannot share,
> Reveres the reverence which it cannot feel. (II, 9)

This same dilemma, expressed in terms of the question of immortality, is again the theme of the sonnet "To One Who Had Written in Derision of the Belief in Immortality." In it Watson's reluctant agnosticism, his emotional desire to believe, is implicit in his words of caution to those who casually and coldly dismiss the age-old belief in immortality:

> Nay, tenderly, if needs thou must, disprove
> My loftiest fancy, dash my grand desire
> To see this curtain lift, these clouds retire,
> And Truth, a boundless dayspring, blaze above
> And round me; and to ask of my dead sire
> His pardon for a word that wronged his love. (II, 20)

Yet despite all the misgivings which Watson had about the future and his longings for the past, his firm commitment to his nation and its future is exhibited in the volume in "To a Friend," a sonnet in which he praised the man who "livest not alone in thoughts outworn,/ But ever helpest the new time be born." Expressing his conservative yet progressive attitude of mind, the poet concluded: ". . . I count him wise,/ Who loves so well Man's noble memories/ He needs must love Man's nobler hopes yet more" (II, 21).

In *Odes and Other Poems* Watson, to be sure, continued his discussion of poetry and the poet. For instance, the Horatian ode "To Arthur Christopher Benson" is an effective restatement of Watson's conception of poetry: an art seriously concerned with the problems of the day expressed in the traditional idiom of the past.

In a similar ode, "To H. D. Traill," Watson continued a theme earlier expressed in the "Prelude" to *Poems*—that poetic inspiration was for him a frustratingly uncertain occurrence. And there can be no doubt but that Watson found his capricious Muse an increasingly serious problem. Consequently, he was not at all averse to a limitless poetic domain. As he expressed it in the ode:

> Whate'er we know, whate'er we dream,
> All things that are, all things that seem,
> All that in Nature's Academe
> Her graduates learn,
> Was Bacon's province, Shakespeare's theme,
> Goethe's concern. (I, 145)

But though the poet is free to take all things as his province, the ideal poem is one in which the real and the ideal, the material and the spiritual, coalesce. In a rare but finely expressed passage, Watson described those moments of transcendent poetic insight which enable the poet to give to his humbly rooted poems their crowning glory:

'Tis from those moods in which Life stands
With feet earth-planted, yet with hands
Stretched toward visionary lands,
Where vapours lift
A moment, and aërial strands
Gleam through the rift,
The poet wins, in hours benign,
At older than the Delphic shrine,
Those intimations faint and fine,
To which belongs
Whatever character divine
Invest his songs.[5]

However, in "The First Skylark of Spring," Watson, again very much the poet of an iron age, lamented his inability to achieve those wonderful moments of insight. Wistfully he longed for the age of gold when man could sing "In porches of the lucent morn,/ Ere he had felt his lack of wing,/ Or cursed his iron bourn" (I, 42–43). The skylark, which functions in the ode as a symbol of the unfettered imagination, the visionary mind of the ideal poet, serves to remind the present-day bard of a bygone age when "springtime bubbled in his throat" and to beckon him

. . . to the dizzy verge,
And lur'st him o'er the dazzling line,
Where mortal and immortal merge,
And human dies divine. (I, 43)

Although Watson seldom if ever attained this kind of Keatsian heaven's bourne, he never tired of conceiving of the poet as a semi-divine being with access to the great secrets of the world. In a poem reminiscent to the Shelleyan bard clebrated in Tennyson's "The Poet," Watson pictured "The Sovereign Poet" sitting "above the clang and dust of Time,/ With the world's secret trembling on his lip" (I, 160). But perhaps his finest expressions of the lofty nature of poetry appeared in *Odes and Other Poems* as a simple quatrain:

Forget not, brother singer! that though Prose
Can never be too truthful or too wise,

Vita Nuova

> Song is not Truth, not Wisdom, but the rose
> Upon Truth's lips, the light in Wisdom's eyes. (II, 105)

Odes and Other Poems received a rather mixed reception from the critics that indicated in some instances a sense of caution and reservation not often encountered heretofore. The *Spectator,* more ecstatic than ever, dared to place Watson above Wordsworth and on an equal par with Tennyson and Milton. In a tone of supreme confidence, the reviewer (probably Hutton) declared Watson to be "the greatest poet still amongst us." Comparing the "Vita Nuova" favorably with the best of Milton's references to his own privations, the critic asserted that the poet was, "Indeed, at least as sure of ear as Tennyson himself." Effusively sprinkling his lengthy discussion of "The First Skylark of Spring" with honorific terms and enthusiastic phrases, the reviewer judged the poem superior to Wordsworth's "To a Skylark" and equal to Shelley's famous lyric.[6]

Like so many others, E. K. Chambers found the skylark lyric to be the best thing in *Odes and Other Poems.* "If Mr. Watson always wrote with this direct magic of intuition one would have little fear for his poetic immortality; but unfortunately," he continued, "it is at present his rarer mood." Finding lack of inspiration a serious flaw in Watson's works, Chambers noted that a paucity of ideas and intuitive insight do not readily appear as blemishes in works embellished with the "fripperies of art"; but, he observed, Watson has deliberately chosen "a manner unadorned and severe." Consequently, when he has nothing to say, nothing conceals the fact.[7] Again a note of reserve was sounded in the *Athenaeum* when the reviewer observed that Watson had learned "more from his masters than he has brought to them. We have read his latest book with real appreciation of its many admirable qualities, but, on closing it," he reflected, "we have no more definite idea of Mr. Watson himself, of what he really is, apart from what he chooses to express, than we had before opening it." [8]

This critical point, in particular, was the center of the *Saturday Review*'s discerning and perceptive criticism entitled "Mr. Watson's New Poems." In many ways the opening gun, so to speak, in the crucial debate concerning Watson's stature as a poet, the *Saturday Review*'s critic, after some choice words of praise, turned to the matter of Watson's debt to Wordsworth, Tennyson, and Arnold. "They have taught him invaluable lessons," he observed, "but there is one lesson which they have not taught him: they have not revealed him to himself. It is impossible to imagine Mr. Watson without Wordsworth, Matthew Arnold, and Tennyson. We admire in him an exquisite accomplishment, but we fail to grasp a new personality; we fail to find a new subject-matter. He seems always to be doing over again, almost as well, what has been already done better." With the *Spectator's* extravagant claims that Watson was a major poet clearly in mind, the critic willingly conceded that the poet had attained distinction, had, indeed, achieved much in the realm of poetry; nevertheless, he felt that Watson had failed to achieve the highest; "to bring something new into literature; to begin over again; to mark a new date in the calendar, from which men will come to reckon."

Attempting to account for Watson's considerable popularity, the reviewer, in this significant appraisal of the poet's claim to greatness, was of the opinion that the kind of "poetry which appeals widely to the average cultivated reader is the poetry which, while it comes in a new voice, is sufficiently like what he has been accustomed to read and admire." With a good deal of perspicacity, he then concluded: "The merit, the defect, the cause of success, in Mr. Watson lie precisely in this: he has not found a new subject-matter, or revealed a new personality; but he has carried on a great tradition, almost faultlessly." [9]

That Watson's mental decline did not signal a diminished reputation was not alone due to the notoriety surrounding his illness but also, in large part, the result of the battle for the laureateship which, as we have seen, began long before Tennyson's death in October, 1892, and continued to the end of 1895. According to Edward Valentine, "The log-rolling which, like a disgraceful funeral game around Tennyson's solemn pyre, preluded the selection of the new poet laureate had the effect of exciting to an unwonted degree the curiosity of the public regarding the new and, for the most part, unknown poets of the day." [10] This singular situation was brought about by the fact that the man whose poetic canon and achievement were far greater than that of any other living English poet, Algernon Charles Swinburne, was obviously not acceptable to Queen Victoria—nor were his seconds, William Morris and George Meredith.[11] As a result, the younger generation of poets reaped most of the benefits of the ephemeral wave of interest in poetry which for the duration of the laureate battle swept over England. And none of the younger poets rose so rapidly to the crest of the wave of public interest and excitement as did William Watson. In fact, the long search for a suitable successor to Tennyson at length turned into a kind of nation-wide debate concerning Watson's stature as a poet. As one critic expressed the problem in retrospect, "It was not over Mr. Austin, but over the merits of Mr. Watson, that the battle for the poet-laureateship really raged." [12] And it was the inability of the critics to resolve the debate conclusively in favor of Watson that ultimately decided his fate.

When the battle commenced in 1892, the fact that Watson had only recently risen to prominence and had produced a relatively slender corpus of poetry weighed against his appointment. Grant Richards once reported that "Lord Bryce (then Mr. Bryce), when his opinion was asked, wrote to the Queen that 'it is hard to select from living poets anyone capable of sustaining the tradition of Wordsworth and Tennyson. . . . Mr. W. Watson has written too little to secure the ear of the cultivated public.' " [13] And even though the Earl of Oxford and Asquith once told Watson that he had "strongly urged" Gladstone to appoint him laureate,[14] Jowett's advice not to act at all proved sufficient for both Gladstone and his successor Lord Rosebery.[15]

Meanwhile, Watson, recovered from his illness, published his *Odes and Other Poems* and kept a steady stream of poetry flowing to his favored journals. Now backed more strongly than ever by H. D. Traill, Grant Allen, and Hutton with the resources of the *Spectator,* and by John Lane with his growing prestige as publisher, Watson became a prominent figure in the leading literary circles of London and the center of an enthusiastic following of his own. One of his ardent young admirers was Grant Richards, who recalled in *Memories of a Misspent Youth* his "own small share in furthering the Watson cult," a group of devotees who soon came to believe that the world was ready to accept their champion "as Tennyson's destined successor." Especially did their hopes soar when "Clement Shorter, that weather-vane of literary fashion, welcomed him [Watson] as of the true lineage. . . ." [16]

As the last year of the battle drew nigh, Watson was once again in a position somewhat similar to his situation at the beginning of 1892—riding another crested wave of fame with the coveted laureateship in sight. In March, 1895, Lord Rosebery, Gladstone's successor, awarded him a Civil List Pension of £100 a year; in April, Watson's famous "Hymn to the Sea" appeared as the opening selection in the *Yellow Book;*[17] and in midyear he left his mother and moved to London where he could pursue his fortunes —social as well as professional—with the utmost advantage. In a résumé of the battle situation as it stood in November, 1895, the author of "Chronicle and Comment" in the *Bookman* noticed that Rosebery's recent attention to Watson definitely indicated the strength of his forces. Centering the article on the battle which the author felt was really being waged over Watson's merits and demerits, the writer was concerned with the fact that the controversy was being embittered by personal hostility between the *Spectator* which, of course, supported Watson, and the *Saturday Review* which violently opposed him.[18] Considering "The Question of the Laureate" on the eve of the appointment, Harry Thurston Peck dismissed Alfred Austin along with Sir Edwin Arnold as "most unsuited for such distinction" and singled out Watson and Kipling as the "two names that deserve much thought, and of which we earnestly hope that one may commend itself to the appointing power." Peck thought that Watson was the better poet of the two, but he went on to decide in favor of Kipling on the grounds that he was more representative of the English-speaking people.[19] Thus as 1895 came to an end, so once again did Watson's hopes. Another year of great promise ended in defeat. On December 31, Lord Salisbury, who had succeeded Rosebery as Her Majesty's first minister, decided "to bestow the laurel on a faithful and busy political scribe, Alfred Austin." [20]

But some months before the laureateship was settled, Watson's brother Robinson and his wife relieved him of the care of his mother in the summer of 1895. This arrangement enabled him, for the first time, to fully partake of the busy, opulent social life which the London of the 1890's afforded. Despite his shy, retiring nature, he became a familiar figure at many a tea party and smoker at John Lane's rooms at G1 Albany. Since he was one of Lane's closest friends in this period, Watson's whole social life seemed, for a time, to revolve about the rising young publisher and his Bodley Head coterie.[21] Since dissolving his partnership with Elkin Mathews and moving across Vigo Street with the Bodley Head under his arm, "Lane's new office," according to the chronicler of Piccadilly, Harry Furniss, had rapidly become "the centre of the modern movement in literature and art." [22] And Watson often found himself, especially from 1895 onward, in the midst of this literary hubbub. At Lane's famous smokers he was one among such celebrities as Henry James, H. G. Wells, Lionel Johnson, Aubrey Beardsley, Max Beerbohm, and many others.[23]

Certainly Watson's social success during these years was due largely to Lane's friendship, a relation based upon the publisher's sincere regard for Watson's poetical abilities. Of all the poets whom Lane published, Watson was undoubtedly his favorite, the one poet whose verses emotionally moved him. It is reported that one evening during a visit to America Lane presented the poet Clarence Stedman with a folio of Watson's poems to read aloud; and, as he listened to the sonnet "Life is still life, not yet the hearth is cold," tears ran down his cheeks.[24]

The glimpses which remain of Watson during these London years show him leading a busy but pleasant life. In the summer of 1895 the famous black-and-white artist, E. H. New, saw a good deal of Watson and sometimes recorded their engagements in his diary: "Dined with Lane and William Watson," he wrote on Wednesday, July 24; then on the following day he entered: "Dined with Lane and William Watson at the 'Cheshire Cheese' . . . and then had a lovely walk along the Embankment to Watson's rooms at Westminster, under the Abbey." [25]

Several reports, too, of Lane's persistent matchmaking for Watson have survived; one, in particular, involved the Bodley Head authoress Evelyn Sharp who was rather amused at her publisher's attempts to play Cupid.[26] And although he failed with Watson, Lane, himself, finally married and carried on his social affairs with even greater éclat. J. Lewis May in *John Lane and the Nineties* describes Lane's brilliant Sunday afternoon receptions at No. 8 Lancaster Gate Terrace and remembers Watson as "a well-favoured, neat-headed man of military aspect in a rather close-fitting suit of grey, and a high stiff collar, sitting bolt upright beside Mrs. Lane as she dispensed tea." [27]

II *Watson and the* Yellow Book

But of all the glimpses of the poet during these prosperous middle years of the 1890's, the most significant one has to do with the sensational events surrounding the arrest of Oscar Wilde in April, 1895. During the previous December, John Lane had launched the now famous *Yellow Book* under the direction of Henry Harland and Aubrey Beardsley. And although the journal included among its authors such conservative artists as Henry James and Watson, and on the insistence of Beardsley excluded Wilde, it soon became suspect among the philistines. Consequently, when Wilde was seen with a yellow book under his arm as he was escorted to the Bow Street station on Friday, April 5, the crowd, gathered to see the spectacle, hastily concluded that it was the *Yellow Book*. Shortly after, a riot was staged in Vigo Street in front of the Bodley Head which was stoned,[28] and Beardsley and the *Yellow Book*—both utterly free of the Wildean taint—were drawn into the center of the uproar which shook London for weeks.[29]

John Lane unfortunately was then in New York on his first visit to America, and the business was in charge of a subordinate. Within a matter of hours, a group of Lane's popular but conservative authors led by Watson cabled the publisher in New York urging him not only to sever all connections with Wilde, whose *Salomé* he had published, but also to dismiss Beardsley from the art editorship of the *Yellow Book*.[30] But before Lane (who was in a state of mystification and anxiety) could get his bearings, he received a second cable signed this time by six important Bodley Head authors who threatened to withdraw their books if the publisher did not suppress Beardsley's work in the fifth volume of the *Yellow Book* and omit Wilde's name from the Lane catalogue. Lane, who had the greatest respect for Beardsley,[31] could do nothing but submit under protest. Consequently, the next issue of the *Yellow Book*, which finally appeared on April 30, 1895, was devoid of Beardsley's art except for the *fin-de-siècle* smiles of those four women who (because of an oversight) presided once more over the table of contents on the back cover.

It is apparent that Watson had for some time been unhappy about the presence of Wilde and Beardsley at Lane's Bodley Head. His attitude toward Wilde, in particular, had been made clear numerous times in the past,[32] especially in his satirical poem, "Lines to Our New Censor," in which Watson scourged not only the esthete but also another pet peeve, France. Provoked into ridicule by Wilde's "decision" to become a French citizen, Watson asked:

> And wilt thou, Oscar, from us flee,
> And must we, henceforth, wholly sever?
> Shall thy laborious *jeux-d'esprit*
> Sadden our lives no more for ever?
>
> And all thy future wilt thou link
> With that brave land to which thou goest?
> Unhappy France! we *used* to think
> She touched, at Sedan, fortune's lowest.[33]

According to the famous novelist and niece of Matthew Arnold, Mrs. Humphry Ward, Watson had been planning a protest when the Wilde affair erupted.[34] And there can be little doubt that Watson welcomed the opportunity to champion the conservative cause and to assert his strength in behalf of the traditional-minded, respectable, and proper authors of the day. He, like so many Victorians, had merely tolerated the *fin-de-siècle* artists and poseurs, and had only waited for the right moment to act. When events and circumstances played into his hands, Watson—backed by Wilfred Meynell, Francis Thompson, Mary Ward, and other "appointed guardians of English morality," as Osbert Burdett dubbed them—[35] moved swiftly and carried all before him. As a sure sign of his significant victory, the first item in the April *Yellow Book* was Watson's "Hymn to the Sea."

An ambitious poem written in elegiac couplets, the "Hymn" for numerous reasons caused a considerable stir when it appeared; and it became a kind of central document in the great debate over Watson's status which flared up in the late spring and sum-

mer of 1895. Persistently overwhelming the reader with enthusiastic encomiums to Watson's incomparable poetical talents, H. D.
Traill and Grant Allen, with the untiring aid of R. H. Hutton
and his *Spectator* and the resources of the *Daily Chronicle* had
continued to boom Watson for the poet-laureateship. Unrestrained
and throwing caution to the winds, these Watsonians provoked
the inevitable: responsible, disinterested critics, unmoved by the
tidal wave of praise, became disgusted and incensed. It was time,
they decided, to ask the public to consider exactly what Mr. Watson's claims were. Long showing signs of restiveness, these critics,
led by the staff of the *Saturday Review,* awaited the right occasion which occurred when the *Spectator,* in an effort to outdo itself, admitted "The Hymn to the Sea" to the realms of immortal
poesy in a special review which appeared during the first week in
May, 1895, only four days after the lyric itself had welcomed the
reading public to the Beardsley-less pages of the April *Yellow
Book.*

Addressing the opening remarks to "Those who still entertain
any doubt whether we have again got a really *great* poet amongst
us," the *Spectator* reviewer directed the gaze of the doubtful "to
the poem which appears in the somewhat uncongenial atmosphere of the new number of the *Yellow Book,*" "The Hymn to the
Sea." Quoting the prelude entire from "Grant, O regal in bounty,
a subtle and delicate largess" to "Youth, irrepressibly fair, wakes
like a wondering rose," the critic concluded: "Only a great poet
could have written that, and the last line seems to us one of the
greatest which even great poets have written. Milton never con-
ceived a more delicate and exquisite symbol of the awakening of
youth to the beauty of a world to which it contributes almost as
much loveliness as it perceives in it, than that 'wondering rose' of
Mr. Watson's." [36]

The major rebuttal to this assertion of Watson's poetic suprem-
acy was entitled "Mr. William Watson, Minor Poet," and the
spokesman for the *Saturday Review* sought to expose, at the
outset, the powerful forces at work behind Watson's soaring reputation. Taking notice of Rosebery's recent gift of a £100 annual
pension to the poet, the critic remarked that Watson had, indeed,
"been fortunate among the younger poets in having to depend on
no mere coterie of logrollers to boom his reputation." Pointing out

the obvious, that Watson "has had for some time a clever journal and a highly respectable weekly paper unreservedly devoted to push his reputation," the spokesman went on to say that, "if Mr. Watson's balloon is now visible in the heaven of fame, the continuous puffing of the 'Daily Chronicle' has supplied much of the lifting power to raise it there."

That H. D. Traill and Grant Allen constantly eulogized Watson "in a shower of superlatives" was, the critic remarked, to be expected of those who were known to do anything "to amuse and interest the public daily by any available means and at any cost." However, he continued, warming to his point, "when Mr. R. H. Hutton takes up his weekly trumpet to herald the triumph of a great poet, we are obliged seriously to consider Mr. Watson's claims to greatness and the grounds on which they are based." Referring to the *Spectator's* praise of "The Hymn to the Sea" as "unmeasured and insane," the reviewer commenced his analysis of the poem by pointing out that Watson's use of the elegiac meter was as pretentious and artificial as his presentation of nature in the poem. Bereft of the "natural magic" one expects of such a subject, the "Hymn," as far as the critic was concerned, was a failure because it lacked the genuine Wordsworthian response to nature—the insight that reveals its life.

After a résumé of Watson's considerable abilities as a critic in verse, the Saturday Reviewer moved into the climactic moment of his essay:

The gist of the matter is that, when tried by the three tests of really great poetry, Mr. Watson is found wanting. The first test may be applied in this question, Can he see and can he interpret Nature? The answer must be an unqualified negative. The second test, briefly, is this, Has he found a new and deeper criticism of life? To this question again the reply must be, No. These are the main tests. To the third test, Is his workmanship faultless, or, at least, competent and careful? A more satisfactory answer could be given; but this alone is not sufficient to entitle a poet to a place in the company of the Immortals. Mr. Watson is a minor poet, and a minor poet it is probable he will remain.[37]

III *Watson's* Apologia

It was upon the firm foundation of the Miltonic tradition in English poetry that Watson based his "Apologia" which he wrote in response to his critics in general and to the *Saturday Review*'s appraisal in particular. Appearing as the last poem in *The Father of the Forest and Other Poems,* published in England on November 7, 1895, it was immediately recognized as an able, sincere statement of the poet's rationale. Obviously offended and hurt by his recent critics' assessment of his shortcomings, Watson in his opening lines referred disdainfully to those who chided him, those who curled

> Superior lips,—because my handiwork,
> The issue of my solitary toil,
> The harvest of my spirit, even these
> My numbers, are not something, good or ill,
> Other than I have ever striven, in years
> Lit by a conscious and a patient aim,
> With hopes and with despairs, to fashion them;
> Or, it may be, because I have full oft
> In singers' selves found me a theme of song,
> Holding these also to be very part
> Of Nature's greatness, and accounting not
> Their descants least heroical of deeds;
> Or, yet again, because I bring nought new,
> Save as each noontide or each Spring is new,
> Into an old and iterative world,
> And can but proffer unto whoso will
> A cool and nowise turbid cup, from wells
> Our fathers digged; and have not thought it
> shame
> To tread in nobler footprints than mine own,
> And travel by the light of purer eyes. (I, 99–100)

Indignantly denying that he "with an ape's ambition" had ever rehearsed the gestures of the great poets of the past, Watson claimed to be a "true descendant" of the royal line of poets whose "lineaments, . . . the signature of ancestry" he hoped would "Leap unobscured, and somewhat of themselves/ In me, their lowly scion, live once more" (I, 101). Standing humbly "In the great shade of his majestic sires," those supreme poets who to him were what Nature was to Wordsworth, Watson recalled his dedication and consecrated service to the high calling of poetry:

Vita Nuova

> . . . I too, with constant heart,
> And with no light or careless ministry,
> Have served what seemed the Voice; and
>   unprofane,
> Have dedicated to melodious ends
> All of myself that least ignoble was. (I, 101–2)

Referring contemptuously to the English *poètes maudits*, he asserted that he at least had ". . . not paid the world/ The evil and the insolent courtesy/ Of offering it my baseness for a gift" (I, 102).

Taking up the charge that his verses lacked passion and vigor, Watson maintained that there was a source of ardor and emotion which transcended that of "Eros' lips," a transcendent moment in which the poet

> . . . rapt from all relation with his kind,
> All temporal and immediate circumstance,
> In silence, in the visionary mood
> That, flashing light on the dark deep, perceives
> Order beyond this coil and errancy,
> Isled from the fretful hour he stands alone
> And hears the eternal movement, and beholds
> Above him and around and at his feet,
> In million-billowed consentaneousness,
> The flowing, flowing, flowing of the world. (I, 102–3)

Fine as this description is of the poet-prophet's moments of divine insight, it strikes one as the only aspect of the "Apologia" that is false. For if Watson ever had such a visionary experience similar to Wordsworth's transcendent moments (which he so obviously attempted to describe here), he never succeeded in embodying it in a poem. Nevertheless, the "Apologia," as a whole, is an excellent expression of Watson's *raison d'être* and his critics and public alike accepted it as an accurate statement of what he could do.[38]

The new but slender volume of 1895 contained four other important poems: the title poem, "The Father of the Forest"; the "Hymn to the Sea"; the rather trite tribute entitled "The Tomb of Burns"; and a sonnet, "The Turk in Armenia" which served as a forerunner to the controversial sonnet series, *The Purple East.* Reminiscent of Tennyson's "The Talking Oak," Watson's Father of the Forest has beheld the pageant of history pass beneath its branches. Indulging a favorite poetic technique of painting vignette-like portraits, Watson in the first part of the poem questioned the aged yew about the many famous personages he possibly had seen. In the second part of the poem, the ancient yew, unable to share his youthful questioner's interest in the noisy pageant of human history, and weary of the seemingly endless cycles "Of wars and tears, and death and love," looks forward to "'The advent of that morn divine'" when all creation moves together toward that "golden end" (I, 114), that "one far-off divine event" toward which Tennyson saw "the whole creation" move.

The famous "Hymn to the Sea," which aroused so much emotion both pro and con, is one of Watson's most artificial, heavily latinate poems. An apostrophe to the sea whose strength and tempestuous moods Watson found analogous to man's nature, the poem in elegiac couplets is, in fact, a kind of Swinburnian paean to the unconquerable spirit of man. Like its predecessor, "The Dream of Man," it pictures "Amorous agonist man" as alternately "pining and striving" and as finding "the glory of life only from love and from war" (I, 35). Chained like the sea within bounds that gall him, man, whom Watson celebrated, is a restless, magnificent titan "Born too great for his ends, never at peace with his goal" (I, 36). But unlike the sea who remains loyal to its mistress, the moon, man has shifted his allegiance and imputes his frailties to Nature. But when both sea and man return to "the matrix of Life," "Man and his littleness perish, erased like an error and cancelled,/ Man and his greatness survive, lost in the greatness of God" (I, 40).

Although the reviews of Watson's volume of 1895 were not wholly favorable,[39] Watson had, nevertheless, come through the "wintry terrors" of his most formidable opposition to date with a very respectable reputation still intact, and, for a poet, with a surprisingly large following. The *Saturday Review*, to be sure, had made its point; but Watson's admirers knew what they wanted, and what they wanted Watson had. Consequently, the poet, at the conclusion of 1895, was at one of the high points of his career, despite the fact that on the last day of the year, he lost the laureateship battle to Austin, the poet whom he once dubbed "laureate of the English seasons." [40]

CHAPTER 6

The Tragic Change

To follow Truth was yesterday
To England's heart the surest way.
—William Watson, "The Tragic Change"

A LTHOUGH there is ample evidence in Watson's earlier poetry of his predilection for espousing unpopular causes and
for speaking out courageously on momentous issues which might
have silenced more cautious men, the controversial nature of
Watson's poetry is most marked in the poems he published over
the ten-year period which extends roughly from 1895 to 1905.
Watson's championing of the anti-government position in his "Ver
Tenebrosum" sonnets and his voicing of the doubts of the post-
Darwinian mind in "The Great Misgiving" had caused relatively
little anxiety among his countrymen because he was then a little-
known poet. But by 1895 when he became immersed in the Armenian controversy and, at the same time, wrote his most clearly
agnostic, religiously pessimistic poems, he was to many the leading poet of the day—a man whose every utterance was immediately given the attention accorded only to the nation's leading
spokesmen.

I The Decade of Controversy

Certainly no other period of Watson's life demonstrates so well
his unselfish devotion to the principles of truth, duty, and justice
as does this decade of controversy which cost him so much and
gained him so little. In late 1895 when the poet-laureateship was
still undecided, Watson published "Craven England," [1] the first
of a series of thirteen sonnets on the Turkish massacres of the Armenians. These sonnets during the next few months were to stir
the English as no other poems had done for many years.

That Watson was willing to ignore the consequences of speaking out sharply against the government on a delicate, critical question of international importance is ample proof of his courage, his fearlessness in the face of powerful opposition when justice, truth, and the honor of England were at stake. From the beginning to the end of his poetic career, Watson was determined that the truth, as his forefathers had perceived it, would be known and that justice must be done. The poet was never more himself than when the bardic elements in him were called forth by momentous events of the day, and he spoke out instinctively, sincerely, often fiercely in the spirit of Isaiah, Milton, and Wordsworth against the waywardness of a nation which had strayed from righteousness.

Although Watson was an ardent supporter of the British Empire and an Imperialist of the Tennysonian type who was convinced of England's intellectual and moral superiority and devoted to the proposition that his nation was obligated to set a high example of virtuous living and right-thinking to the world, he was not the kind of Imperialist who saw in England's physical might the immediate opportunity of exploiting the resources of backward nations for materialistic gain. In one of his sonnets of 1885, "Our Eastern Treasure," Watson had clearly indicated his pride in the Empire of the Queen; but, as the callously aggressive, jingoistic spirit of Imperialism began to clearly assert itself in the early 1890's, Watson found himself wholly at odds with its selfish, materialistic orientation, and especially its bellicose tendencies. His fear of where the race for colonies and the wholesale exploitation of human life and physical resources would lead was voiced in those prophetic sonnets, "The World in Armour"; and his earnest, almost feverish attempt to keep English Imperialism true to the dictates of honor, duty, and justice was embodied in the three volumes of political poems of this decade, *The Purple East, The Year of Shame,* and *For England.*

The first of these volumes, *The Purple East,* contained a number of sonnets written mostly in 1895–96 in which Watson attacked the brutal, heathen savagery of the Sultan of Turkey and the apparent apathy and moral decay of England. News of the Turkish Sultan's indulgence in one of his favorite sports, the massacre of minorities within his greatly reduced empire, had reached England in July, 1894.[2] And although the savagery of the Turks had shocked the civilized world before, the massacres of the helpless Armenians and the unbelievable cruelties perpetrated against Christian people within an apparently godless nation aroused the English to an incredible pitch of emotional intensity—and no one was more concerned and outraged than William Watson. On March 2, 1895, while Lord Kimberley, the foreign secretary, was doing everything short of committing England to single-handed military intervention in Turkey, Watson published the sonnet "The Turk in Armenia" in which his impatience with English temporizing was thus early manifest. But Watson was to call England to action and to deplore her hesitant state of mind many times during the next two years; for although the English nation was genuinely in sympathy with its Armenian brethren, the refusal of Russia to sanction armed intervention and the despicable attitude of Germany in actually aiding and abetting the Sultan in order to gain England's heretofore preferred position at Constantinople divided the nation upon the question of intervening alone or of continuing efforts to get the great powers to act together to remedy the outrageous situation.

On December 16, 1895, Watson's widely read, extremely influential series of sonnets began to appear in the *Westminster Gazette* and were published on January 24, 1896, in a little paperbound volume entitled *The Purple East: A Series of Sonnets on England's Desertion of Armenia*. The frontispiece was a representation of the "Recording Angel" by G. F. Watts, R. A., done in a crimson tint. On the same day, most of these sonnets were published in the New York *Times*. Likening England to the Lady in *Comus* who sits, the victim of an evil wand, with her nerves "Chained up in alabaster," Watson, in his Preface, showed his growing sense of disillusionment about England when he wrote that "if an appeal to the national conscience is vain, let us fall back for a moment upon lower ethical considerations, and ask ourselves whether in the end it will even *advantage* us to have postponed the rescue of a dying people to our own alleged interests in the maintenance of a diabolical tyranny. To have been the accessory to a tremendous crime, whether before or after the fact," he then warned the English, "will not permanently aid a nation, . . ." What happens to a people who will not rise with vigor and assurance to protect the right and to chastise the wrong? "Her walk grows feverish, and her rejoicings troubled, for a shadowy accuser waylays her footsteps, and haunts the background of her feasts." Although he simultaneously belabored England's apathetic attitude toward the recurring massacres and the Sultan's hellish pursuits, it was his own country's shameful procrastination which dominated Watson's thoughts in *The Purple East*. England's actions in the present crisis were, in his estimation, but another sign of decadence and decline.

The severest kind of rebuke is voiced in "Craven England," a sonnet which rings with the kind of denunciation once heard in Milton's "On the Massacres in Piemont":

> Never, O craven England, nevermore
> Prate thou of generous effort, righteous aim!
> Betrayer of a people, know thy shame!
> Summer hath passed, and Autumn's threshing-floor
> Been winnowed; Winter at Armenia's door
> Snarls like a wolf; and still the sword and flame
> Sleep not; *thou only* sleepest; and the same
> Cry unto heaven ascends as heretofore;
> The guiltless perish, and no man regards;
> And sunk in ease, and lost to noble pride,
> Stirred by no clarion blowing loud and wide,
> Thy sons forget what Truth and Honour meant,
> And, day by day, to sit among the shards
> Of broken faith are miserably content.

Again and again in "The Knell of Chivalry," "A Hurried Funeral" (which depicts the burial of "England's Honour"), and "A Wondrous Likeness," Watson lashed the English; and in "The Plague of Apathy" the bard spoke out against what seemed to him the one greatest obstacle to a righteous course. As the first wave of emotion and tears subsided, "Indifference like a dewless night" closed over the nation. And with the realization that the "multitude stand dumb" while only the "unconcerned" flourish, Watson's growing conviction that "The England that we vaunted is no more" came upon him with redoubled force.

But pessimistic though *The Purple East* sonnets are, the poet in "Last Word" suggested that England could yet arise and reclaim her nobleness of purpose and flee the things which were degrading her. "Still in your midst," he pointed out,

> . . . there dwells a remnant, who
> Love not an unclean Art, a Stage no less
> Unclean, a gibing and reviling Press,
> A febrile Muse, and Fiction febrile too.
> And they it is would pluck you from the slime
> Whereof the rank miasma clouds your brain
> With sloth that slays and torpor that is crime
> Till ye can feel nought keenly, see nought plain.
> Hearken their call, and heed, while yet is time,
> Lest ye be lulled too deep to wake again.

Watson's series, as one can imagine, provoked a great and varied response. Indeed, his speaking out so strongly against the government in a time of crisis cost him many readers and friends and earned for him the name of a hot-head and reckless meddler. Soon after the sonnets began to appear in the *Westminster Gazette,* Watson's friend and one-time patron, Alfred Austin, the Poet Laureate, published three sonnets, "A Vindication of England," in which he accused Watson of being unpatriotic and attempted to defend the Conservative government's position.[3] Watson's formal reply to the poet laureate appeared as two sonnets, "The Bard-in-Waiting" and "Leisured Justice," which were printed in *The Purple East* volume. Stigmatizing Austin as "Treachery's apologist," Watson, in "The Bard-in-Waiting," asked: "Because I crouch not fawning slaves among,/How is my service proved the less sincere?" If it were not for the love he bore England's "lofty ways," he pointed out, "What were to me her stumblings and her slips?"

Although there were many who shared Watson's attitude toward the Armenian crisis, there were many more who did not. Many reviewers, for instance, ignored *The Purple East,* and those who condescended to speak of it had little to say in its favor. Even Watson's staunchest literary supporter, the *Spectator,* which had always been with him when he was cautious and conservative, sided with the opposition and rebuked him (as lightly as the task could be managed) for treading out of bounds. "We believe with Mr. Watson that the responsibility of inaction is very great," the reviewer wrote. "But we are quite sure that the responsibility of bringing these immense armed hosts into collision would have been frightful also. It is hardly for a poet, hardly even a journalist," the critic pointed out, "to measure these half-seen, half-hidden, but gigantic responsibilities." [4] Not so confident as Watson that the Armenians could be saved without provoking a clash of arms between the great powers, the spokesman for the *Spectator* reminded the poet that neither he nor anyone else outside the government was "in the position from which any clear judgment can be confidently formed." Again employing what the reviewer found to be a useful syntax, he continued, "We heartily sympathize with Mr. Watson's indignation, but we are disposed to think that very few statesmen have ever existed even in England, who would not have shrunk from giving the word which might have drowned all Europe in blood." Although the critic did not feel that Watson's "fine sonnets" would detract from his reputation as a poet, he believed that the poems would certainly not add to it. This, too, was the opinion of the spokesman for the *Nation* who denied the sonnets that "double crown of heroism and poetic triumph" which some of Milton's political sonnets attained.[5]

Despite the widespread opposition, Watson continued to urge his cause with sonnets to the newspapers such as the *Daily Chronicle* and the New York *Times* in the pages of which appeared "To the Sultan," the most famous of his Armenian poems, in late January, 1896. Crowning the Turkish ruler "with the brightest of Hell's aureoles," Watson also bestowed upon the potentate the epithet "Abdul the Damned," which immediately became one of the favorite phrases of the day. An indication of this poem's popularity was W. Alison Phillips' cartoon in the pages of *Punch* which depicted an astonished Sultan "reading to himself from his presentation copy of Mr. William Watson's sonnets." Seated upon the floor and deluged with volumes of Watson's poetry and copies of *Daily Chronicles*, His Imperial Majesty—under the watchful eye of Watts's "The Recording Angel"—exclaimed: "Well, I'm——! I mean, Bismillah!" [6] The poem also struck Max Beerbohm's fancy and suggested to him an amusing caricature of Watson (who had been "secretly ceded by the British government to Abdul Hamid") being spirited away—mustache and all—by a giant fezzed Turk. Fortunately for Watson there was John Lane in the background down upon his knees passionately interceding with a fierce, implacable potentate who "in the nick of time" relents to save the poet "from the trap-door to the Bosphorus." [7]

By December, 1896, Watson had gathered together sixteen of the *Purple East* sonnets and ten new poems and had published them in a volume called *The Year of Shame* with a long introduction by the Bishop of Hereford. Widely read and much talked about, this work brought together in final form Watson's best efforts in behalf of the Armenian cause. Described as "moral tonics" designed to revive in the English the spirit of justice and honor, the sonnets in *The Year of Shame* were, according to the bishop's preface, written in "the spirit of Isaiah," a spirit which warned the English "that behind those desolated Armenian homes, those tortured and murdered men, those dishonoured and heart-broken women, there stands the vision of a stern and unavoidable reckoning for those who might have saved and would not or dared not."

The *Bookman* critic who reviewed *The Year of Shame* also noticed the passionate utterance and the prophetic tone, and admitted that the sonnets were "obvious preaching." But since he was more concerned with the literary quality of the sonnet series, he went on to assure those "thinking primarily of form, diction, art," that "the work satisfies and delights. How exceeding rare it is," he exclaimed, "to find purpose poetry—for such it may fairly enough be called—rising to such a level." Although the Armenian sonnets were to his way of thinking the "spontaneous product of a poetic nature deeply moved," the reviewer felt that the final appeal of "this slender fascicule of verse" would be literary and, as a consequence, would "stand the test—the eternal test—of beauty." [8]

During the time Watson was feverishly writing his Armenian sonnets, he was at work on several other poems which—although equally as controversial—were concerned with what might be described as philosophical subjects demanding more mental concentration and conscious artistry.

II The Hope of the World

Having appeared in various newspapers and journals since the spring of 1896, these poems, including some notable lyrics, were gathered together in one of Watson's most significant and controversial volumes, *The Hope of the World and Other Poems*, published in December, 1897. The title poem along with "The Unknown God," "Ode in May," and "The Lost Eden" constitute the most important statement of Watson's attitude toward God and the destiny of man. In these poems his characteristic responses to the great enigmas of existence are most clearly formulated.

From the *Prince's Quest* volume on, Watson had shown his great interest in the nature of God in such poems as "God-Seeking" and "The Questioner"; his concern for man's destiny in "The Blind Summit" and "The Dream of Man"; and his skeptical bent of mind in "The Great Misgiving," "To Aubrey De Vere," and "To One Who Had Written in Derision of the Belief in Immortality." And although his religious attitude was seemingly somewhat protean in that it often wavered or changed, his responses were throughout his life characteristically Watsonian; and they were conditioned by the particular time in which he lived and by the makeup of his own personality. During his earler years as a poet, the unorthodox religious views expressed in his poems passed almost unnoticed, mixed in as they were with other poems which conveyed seemingly orthodox notions. It was not until *The Hope of the World* appeared that Watson's unorthodoxy—his pessimistic, rather wistful agnosticism—made its full impact on his readers and stirred up a considerable reaction.

From the beginning, there were two major factors which conditioned Watson's response to the ultimate questions of life: the simple, pious orthodoxy derived from his mother's religious teachings, and the agnosticism and receptivity of mind toward scientific knowledge instilled in him by his father. The mingling of these two inimical influences in his mind during his early years prevented him from being either a devout Christian or what one might call a comfortable agnostic. His was the typical dilemma of many late Victorians who had been born and reared in what the poet called the lost Eden wherein man "dreamed himself the first/ Of creatures, fashioned for eternity," but who now found himself in an alien world, beset by doubts and griefs he previously knew not of. For Watson the dilemma resulted in a sad, reluctant kind of agnosticism which enabled him—longing as he did for the old assurances, yet intellectually committed to a repugnant philosophy—to express himself at times like a thorough atheist and at other times like an orthodox Christian.

Watson's sympathy for the old faith and his emotional need for the affirmations it afforded are evidenced in poems which occurred throughout his life such as "To Aubrey De Vere" (1894), "On the Author's Fifty-Fifth Birthday" (1913), and "Cross Brow, Ambleside" (1921), poems in which their author's emotional allegiance to Christianity is manifest. But Watson's reluctant acquiescence to the evidences of recent scientific developments made it intellectually impossible for him to give credence longer to the tenets of the Christian religion whose God he so often continued to invoke. That his characteristic attitude of mind was unquestionably that of the post-Darwinian is evidenced in all his major poetic statements of creed. In addition, Watson, on several occasions throughout his life, stated his position in respect to religion as he did, for instance, in a letter which he wrote to Edmund Gosse in 1917. Discussing how his upbringing had differed from that of Gosse as described in *Father and Son,* Watson declared that he had come "directly under Darwinian influence at an early age, and had quite thrown off all orthodoxy in religion &c. before I was even approaching my last teens." [9]

In "The Hope of the World," a poem whose tone and mood as well as its stanzaic form owe much to Empedocles' first long soliloquy in Arnold's *Empedocles on Etna,* Watson in a characteristically somber, pessimistic mood, subjected man's grounds for hope to a withering analysis. In particular he focussed upon the most prevalent optimistic philosophies of life: the Christian doctrine of love, and a kind of Spencerian optimism popular at the time which taught that evolution inevitably meant progress. Gazing about him with an intellectual eye unobscured by emotion, the poet looked in vain for evidences of love except in man's heart alone. In the spirit of Empedocles, he asked: if Love dwells "in homes of men,/ In hearts that crave and die./ Dwells he not also, then,/ With Godhead, throned on high?" With grim emphasis, he was compelled to answer:

> This and but this I know:
> His face I see not there:

> Here find I him below,
> Nor find him otherwhere;
> Born of an aching world, Pain's bridegroom,
> Death's ally. (I, 123)

Not only was the universe amoral, often ruthless—"red in tooth and claw," as Tennyson expressed it—but it was for Watson devoid of any sure sign

> That through all Nature's frame
> Boundless ascent benign
> Is everywhere her aim,
> Such as man hopes it here,
> Where he from beasts hath risen,—
> (I, 123–24)

It would be comforting, indeed, to know

> That Earth, from primal bloom,
> With pangs of prescient bliss
> Divined us in her womb;
> That fostering powers have made
> Our fate their secret care,
> And wooed us, grade by grade,
> Up winding stair on stair.

But, wrote the poet, "not for golden fancies iron truths make room." [10]

In a series of stanzas of poetic statement, Watson then traced the evolution of man:

> In cave and bosky dene
> Of old there crept and ran
> The gibbering form obscene
> That was and was not man. (I, 124)

Less beautiful and well-appointed than birds and other beasts, man by "some random throw/ Of heedless Nature's die" rose from this unpromising situation to his present ascendance. Emphasizing what so many of his optimistic contemporaries seemed to

The Tragic Change

overlook, Watson pointed out that no purposeful force guided man's ascent; rather it

> 'Twould seem he climbed at last
> In mere fortuitous hour,
> Child of a thousand chances 'neath the
> indifferent sky.
> A soul so long deferred
> In his blind brain bore,
> It might have slept unstirred
> Ten million noontides more.
> Yea, round him Darkness might
> Till now her folds have drawn,
> O'er that enormous night
> So casual came the dawn,
> Such hues of hap and hazard Man's Emergence wore!
> (I, 125–26)

If chance has played so large a part in man's development, Watson concluded,

> What ground is mine to assume
> An upward process *there,*
> In yonder worlds that shine
> From alien tracts of sky?
> Nor ground to assume is mine
> Nor warrant to deny.
> Equal, my source of hope, my reason for despair. (I, 126)

In this his best statement of his belief that there is no guarantee that there is either a God or a vital, purposeful life-force which makes for the inevitable rise of man to ever higher heights of intelligence and material comfort, Watson suggested that modern man's most honest, intelligent course was to see life as it really is and to accept it on its own terms. All man knows is that his present state is the result of a blind, amoral, irresistible force pushing all living things along an undetermined path. It is in a way tragic, Watson felt, that man by pure chance has developed a mind which has become aware of itself, a mind which reasons and conceives of love as being the highest law of life and yet remains subject to a mindless force which treats man like all other animate and inanimate objects, baffling and crushing him with absolutely no regard for his superior mental and spiritual powers. But "loath to suffer mute," in the words of Arnold's Empedocles,

> We, peopling the void air,
> Make Gods to whom to impute
> The ills we ought to bear;
> With God and Fate to rail at, suffering easily.

Unlike so many of his late nineteenth-century contemporaries, Watson rejected this course as ignoble. Instead, he resisted the tempting voice of Hope which subtly whispered its tales of God-ward progress and of life after death in his ear, and concluded with a vigorous assertion of his rather somber, stoic attitude. Here on this earth alone where perhaps

> I conquer or I fail.
> Here, o'er the dark Deep blown,
> I ask no perfumed gale;
> I ask the unpampering breath
> That fits me to endure
> Chance, and victorious Death,
> Life, and my doom obscure,
> Who know not whence I am sped, nor to
> what port I sail. (I, 129–30)

Watson's attitude toward inevitable progress stated in "The Hope of the World" is in one respect but another illustration of his basically pessimistic view of life—of his deep inward suspicion of any naïvely exuberant scheme of progress. In *The Eloping Angels* Watson humorously had presented a happy-go-lucky Faust cockily preaching the popular nineteenth-century doctrine of aspiration, but in its more serious counterpart, "The Dream of Man," [11] the poet, satirizing modern man's confidence in his ability to conquer all ills and to remove all obstacles, indicated that striving itself would never bring what one might call ultimate happiness—perfect bliss and repose. For, in the poem the goal of man once attained was found specious: the very act of striving, which in itself is painful, turned out to be the highest happiness man could attain. That striving would not bring either peace or truth is, in "The Blind Summit," made abundantly clear in a statement which seems to me to be an excellent expression of the poet's true response to the philosophical attitude so often identified with Browning:

> So mounts the child of ages of desire,
> Man, up the steeps of Thought; and would behold
> Yet purer peaks, touched with unearthlier fire,
> In sudden prospect virginally new;
> But on the lone last height he sighs: ' 'Tis cold,
> And clouds shut out the view.' (I, 118)

In the two poems which follow "The Hope of the World"— "The Unknown God" and "Ode in May"—Watson presented in clear, unmistakable terms the two salient features of his attitude toward God which remain constant throughout his work—the notion that, if God exists, he is too obscured by the veil of materiality to be knowable in any useful sense, and that the only evidence for his existence is the rhythmic pulsations manifest in the orderly motions of nature. Admitting that at times he felt "a sense of God," Watson in "The Unknown God" rejected the Biblical notion of the deity—"Man's giant shadow, hailed divine"—as being incompatible with the scant evidence man has of His nature. Certainly, Watson did not find his sense of God or the manifestations of Him in the universe to be enough upon which to base a sound religious system. Expressing his idea of deity in its most characteristic form, the poet, using the mystic words or sayings of Jesus discovered at Oxyrhynchus in 1897,[12] wrote:

> The God I know of, I shall ne'er
> Know, though he dwells exceeding nigh.
> *Raise thou the stone and find me there,*
> *Cleave thou the wood and there am I.*
> Yea, in my flesh his spirit doth flow,
> Too near, too far, for me to know. (I, 132)

So hidden beneath the surface of things, so inscrutable were the ways of his God, that Watson could not be sure his deeds could either "pleasure him or vex"; and, as he went on to express it,

> . . . dreaming much, I never dare
> To dream that in my prisoned soul
> The flutter of a trembling prayer
> Can move the Mind that is the Whole. (I, 133)

Summarizing his conceptions of his enigmatic diety, the poet concluded:

> Unmeet to be profaned by praise
> Is he whose coils the world enfold;
> The God on whom I ever gaze,
> The God I never once behold:
> Above the cloud, beneath the clod:
> The Unknown God, the Unknown God. (I, 134)

This being of Watson's who appeared earlier in "Wordsworth's Grave" as ". . . that secluded Spirit unknowable,/ The mystery we make darker with a name" (I, 17) is the pantheistic deity, that "spirit divine/ Of universal loveliness" to whom Tennyson's soul returned in Watson's "Lachrymae Musarum"—a divine force which is, in fact, similar to Tennyson's own concept in the "Higher Pantheism."

This notion of a primal life-force, immutable and eternal, from which all life returns, is celebrated in the joyous "Ode in May," a kind of pagan chant—rhythmical, melodious, and optimistic— found more often in the pages of Swinburne and Meredith.[13] Untypical of Watson in its untroubled, wholehearted paganism, the "Ode" is reminiscent of the second chorus in Swinburne's *Atalanta in Calydon* which, like Watson's poem, celebrates the "making of man" in a rhythmical, chant-like stanza form.

Interesting as these poems are, and finely as they express major aspects of the poet's typical response to the ultimate questions of life, Watson's most characteristic and compelling depiction of man alone in the post-Darwinian universe is the poem entitled, "The Lost Eden," which appeared originally as the opening selection in the *Yellow Book* for January, 1897.[14] Considerably different in form from "The Lost Eden" published in *The Hope of the World* volume, the poem, nevertheless, expresses the same thought: that man was expelled from Eden when scientific knowledge reached the point where the revelations of the Christian faith were no longer tenable. Once again satirizing man's high but unrealistic opinion of himself, the poet in both versions of the poem pictured man exulting in his special position in the scheme of things as the crown of creation; "So in an Eden/ Dwelt he, of fantasies" (*Yellow Book* version, 12). But within man was that passion for forbidden knowledge, that desire to be as gods which, as in Milton's *Paradise Lost*, is objectified in the poem in the form of Eve—

> Eve the hot-hearted!
> Eve the wild spirit
> Of quest—the adventurer!
> Eve the unslaked.
> She it was showed him
> Where, in the midst
> Of his pleasance, the knowledge-tree
> Waiting him grew.
> (*Yellow Book*, 13)

The most interesting aspect of the poem, of course, is not so much the description of man before the "imperative world-thirst drave him forth" from his home of innocent happiness, as it is the depiction of modern man who has sent "His spirit abroad among the infinitudes,/ And may no more to the ancient pales recall/ The travelled feet" (I, 117). In the concluding lines of the poem, Watson expressed in a Ulysses-like figure (reminiscent of Tennyson's great aspirer) all the wistfulness and the tragedy he saw in the human condition in an alien, Darwinian world. Despite all his new-won knowledge, man oftentimes ". . . feels/ The intolerable vastness bow him down,/ The awful homeless spaces daunt his soul" (I, 117); then it is that, half regretful, he remembers

> His Eden lost, as some grey mariner
> May think of the far fields where he was bred,
> And woody ways unbreathed-on by the sea,
> Though more familiar now the ocean-paths
> Gleam, and the stars his fathers never knew. (I, 117)

This poem is an excellent indication of Watson's attitude toward recent scientific developments and in particular toward Darwin's discoveries. Despite Watson's obvious relish in telling about his early acceptance of the doctrine of evolution, and proud as he was to have written to Darwin and to have received from the great man perhaps the last letter he wrote before his death, Watson despised and distrusted the scientists' insatiable thirst for knowledge and their proud confidence in their own abilities.[15] Without doubt, Watson's congenital melancholy was intensified by his inability to overcome the damnable knowledge of science and to return to the serene world of the age of faith when God was in his heaven and all was right with the world.

To a man as sensitive and compassionate as Watson was, his considered view of modern man's place in the scheme of things was a constant source of depression and melancholy. Longing to be a free spirit soaring into the blue heaven of Divine Love, he found himself a mortal "fettered to the sod" where, as he said in "The First Skylark of Spring," ". . . fruitless knowledge clouds my soul,/ And fretful ignorance irks it more" (I, 42). Only in those somber sonnets of unrelieved gloom, "Night on Curbar Edge" and "Melancholia," is the dark night of William Watson's soul fully revealed—sonnets in which his attitude toward life expressed in *The Hope of the World* poems is symbolized by a barren, desolate earth. Filled with echoes of Arnold's "Dover Beach," these sonnets, like "The Hope of the World," reveal how strongly Arnold's poetic representations of the modern world appealed to Watson. In "Melancholia," in which he pictured himself standing "In the cold starlight, on the barren beach" alone, the poet, like Arnold before him,

> . . . heard the long hiss of the backward wave
> Down the steep shingle, and the hollow speech
> Of murmurous cavern-lips, nor other breach
> Of ancient silence. (II, 24)

Almost overwhelmed by the terrible vision of the universe's hostility to man, he stood desolate beneath the arch of "everlasting taciturnity": "The august, inhospitable, inhuman night,/ Glittering magnificently unperturbed (II, 24).

Again depressed by the evidence that science gives of nature's carelessness of man, Watson in "Night on Curbar Edge" described a place like Hardy's Egdon Heath "which had slipped out of its century generations ago to intrude as an uncouth object into this." An objectification of that center of desolation and melancholy deep within himself, Curbar Edge stands in a region

> Where time by aeons reckons, not by years.
> Its patient form one crag, sole stranded, rears,
> Type of whate'er is destined to remain
> While yon still host encamped on night's waste plain
> Keeps armèd watch, a million quivering spears. (II, 3)

The gloom of *The Hope of the World* volume is somewhat lessened by the poet's most famous lyric, "April, April," which even today remains in the memory of many who learned it in school during the early years of this century. Light, lilting, and gay, it is, like most of Watson's songs, slight but memorable:

> April, April,
> Laugh thy girlish laughter;
> Then, the moment after,
> Weep thy girlish tears!
> April, that mine ears
> Like a lover greetest,
> If I tell thee, sweetest,
> All my hopes and fears,
> April, April,
> Laugh thy golden laughter,
> But, the moment after,
> Weep thy golden tears! (I, 89)

Although his volumes almost always contained a few lyrics, most of them were like "April, April": rather conventional in theme and form with little of the subtle complexity and deep emotion characteristic of the best English lyrics. Occasionally, as in "Thy voice from inmost dreamland calls," the poet rather successfully imitated the Tennysonian lyrics from *The Princess*. And once he achieved a notable success with the unrhymed lyric— "England My Mother," a poem in which the short two-beat lines provided an appropriate rhythmical setting for his celebration of the poet's art.[16] Relating the rhythm and harmony of poetry to the "choric/ Chant of creation," Watson indicated the high regard he had for his craft when he wrote:

> God on His throne is
> Eldest of poets:
> Unto His measures
> Moveth the Whole. (I, 67)

In addition to "April, April," *The Hope of the World* volume contained several poems which call attention to the fact that they were written at a time when Watson was still intensely absorbed in various European political situations, especially that in Greece. His preoccupation with troubles upon the Continent not only revealed itself in whole poems such as "Hellas, Hail!" but also obtruded in "The Unknown God" in the form of a rebuttal to Kipling's "Recessional." Echoing the famous lines, "Lord God of Hosts, be with us yet,/ Lest we forget—lest we forget!," Watson wrote:

> Best by remembering God, say some,
> We keep our high imperial lot.
> Fortune, I fear, hath oftenest come
> When we forgot—when we forgot!
> A lovelier faith their happier crown,
> But history laughs and weeps it down! (I, 133)

Bitter and depressed over England's response to the Armenian situation, the poet went on in his *Year of Shame* mood to declare:

> Know they not well, how seven times seven,
> Wronging our mighty arms with rust,
> We dared not do the work of heaven
> Lest heaven should hurl us in the dust?
> The work of heaven! 'Tis waiting still
> The sanction of the heavenly will. (I, 134)

These blasphemous lines which shocked his public indicate that the events which occurred as a result of the Armenian mas-

sacres did much to disillusion Watson and to prove to him beyond
a doubt that a god of love did not exist. Certainly his recent and
unsuccessful efforts in behalf of the Armenians influenced the
openness with which the poet expressed his religious attitude in
The Hope of the World, a volume in which his conviction that the
Christian God of love did not exist was stated more forcefully and
directly than it had been in the *Purple East* sonnet, "A Trial of
Orthodoxy," which by indirection suggested as much:

> What wonder if yon torn and naked throng
> Should doubt a Heaven that seems to wink and nod,
> And having moaned at noontide, 'Lord, how long?'
> Should cry, 'Where hidest Thou?' at evenfall,
> At midnight, 'Is He deaf and blind, our God?'
> And ere day dawn, 'Is He indeed at all?' (II, 57)

Declaring flatly that "The Unknown God" had become "the subject of more criticism and comment, doubtless, than have greeted
any occasional poem since Tennyson's 'Locksley Hall Sixty Years
After,'" Adelene Wicks in her discourse on Watson's poems came
very close to expressing the truth; for the major poems in *The
Hope of the World* did shock the orthodox into a considerable response.[17] The *Spectator* which had of late found it increasingly
difficult to go along with the poet's radical political views, was no
happier about his unorthodox religious notions. Admitting that
"The Unknown God" was "marked with the thoughtfulness, the
power of language, and the harmony of sound which mark all his
poetic work," the reviewer frankly stated at the outset that "With
the intention of the poem we are, and believe most of his readers
will be, entirely out of sympathy."[18] Looking at *The Hope of the
World* as a reflection of the times, H. D. Traill in his review mar-
velled at how far the English had "travelled from the tremulous
optimism of the middle Victorian era, and into how much bleaker
and barer a region of thought than that within which the poetic
speculations of Tennyson were confined! However 'faintly' the
poet of 'In Memoriam' trusted 'the larger hope,' he did trust
it, . . ." Watson's "The Hope of the World," he continued, "appears eight-and-thirty years after it [Darwin's *Origin of Species*],
and, familiar as is the commonplace that the doctrine of evolution

has revolutionized modern thought, it derives a new and almost startling vividness from a comparison of these two poems." [19]

Early in 1899 Watson inherited a considerable sum of money—over ten thousand pounds—from his uncle, William Robinson, whom he had accompanied to Madeira several years before. Relieved for the first time since his father's death from the task of making a living by writing, the poet from all indications took advantage of the respite and led a more restless life than usual; he traveled about from seacoast resorts to Lake Country inns but usually avoided London which always vexed him. Between *The Hope of the World* and another slender volume of verse (most of which had appeared from time to time in newspapers or journals) entitled *For England*, Watson published nothing during a period of six years save the poem which sustained (or should I say redeemed) his reputation, the "Ode on the Day of the Coronation of King Edward the Seventh."

III *The Coronation Ode*

Although Queen Victoria had died on January 22, 1901, the coronation of Edward, long delayed, was finally set for June 27, 1902. In anticipation of the event, Watson began work on his ode in March, and completed it in time for publication on June 13. Because of his recent political opinions and unorthodox religious sentiments, subscriptions for the "Ode" were far below expectations, and John Lane cut down on the first printing. However, the "Ode" was immediately popular and within a matter of days a second printing of four thousand copies had to be made. But, unfortunately, no sooner had this been done when Edward became ill with acute appendicitis and the coronation was postponed until August. Sales not only immediately fell, but Watson insisted on a new printing in which the lines: "High on the noon and summit of the year/ Thou art anointed king" would be omitted. In their place, the following lines were to be substituted to make the "Ode" coincide with the new date of the coronation:

> Lo, at the Earth's high feast, ere Autumn bring
> His afterthoughts on greatness to her ear,
> And with monitions of mortality

> Perturb the revelling year,
> Thou goest forth and art anointed King. (II, 97)

Watson's desire for this emendation precipitated an altercation with Lane (just one of a number of disputes and misunderstandings which increased over the years until Lane chose to cease dealing with the poet altogether). Finally, the two men decided to have Henry Norman, a mutual friend, decide the dispute, which he did, in favor of Lane, and the affair came to an end.[20]

Despite this unpleasantness, the "Ode" proved one of Watson's happiest efforts, drawing almost universal praise from reviewers and eliciting letters of congratulation from many important people. For instance, Thomas Hardy on June 30, 1902, wrote to Watson: "I will not attempt to criticize. All I can say is that the Ode struck me on a first reading, & still impresses me, as being a piece of your very highest work; & to reach the level of your former productions is no mean achievement. Ideas & execution are singularly sustained throughout. I cannot find any place where they dip or falter: & my regret at coming to the last page was that there was no more of the poem." [21]

Calling attention in passing to the fact that Watson had "been poetically silent of late years," the reviewer for the *Academy* was pleased to find the poet "early in the field on the subject of the Coronation; and with remarkable success." Going on to explain his point, the critic wrote: "Remarkable; because the very words 'Coronation Ode' sound dismally in the ears of all who love poetry. They suggest the perfunctory dutifulness of Laureates, the frosty enthusiasm of loyal versifiers who seize a conventional occasion for self-advertisement and the pocketing of a modest fee; exercises in which Pegasus evidently prances under a free use of the spur." Yet the critic pointed out that Watson, like Shakespeare, handled the occasional theme in one of the two ways it could be properly and felicitously done: by the "mingling of noble eloquence and noble rhetoric, just shot with poetry, and couched in raised poetic diction; so that the whole admixture, without attaining absolute poetry, mere poetry (in the Roman phrase), is lifted far above the loftiest strain tolerable in prose." [22]

Like "Wordsworth's Grave" and "Lachrymae Musarum," the

"Coronation Ode" is, as most of the reviewers pointed out, typical
of Watson at his best and—I might add—at his most characteristic. He would have been an appropriate laureate for the closing
years of Victoria's reign, carrying on in Tennyson's stead the kind
of traditional verse the queen and so many of her loyal subjects
loved so well. Certainly in the "Coronation Ode" Watson revealed
the qualities which would have made him the most appropriate
poet laureate in the 1890's. He was the one poet of the time who
could have carried on the public's notion of what laureate poetry
should be: a poetry of lofty, unexceptionable sentiments, clear
and intelligible to all despite its majestic, often Miltonic syntax
and its latinate diction; poetry which through its heightened language and patriotic, pious effusions brought tears to the eyes of
the meek, touched the hearts of the common laborer, comforted
the poor; filled the rich and powerful with a sense of well-being;
and aroused in all a feeling of pride and devotion to God and
country.

Moved for the moment to forget the "Craven England" which
had failed the suffering Armenians, Watson's pride in his great nation found frequent and often eloquent expression in the "Ode."
Rejoicing in the great Empire, Watson in the first strophe exclaimed:

> Time, and the ocean, and some fostering star,
> In high cabal have made us what we are,[23]
> Who stretch one hand to Huron's bearded pines,
> And one on Kashmir's snowy shoulder lay,
> And round the streaming of whose raiment shines
> The iris of the Australasian spray. (II, 95)

Recalling the mighty kings of England's illustrious past and describing in festive mood the splendors of the day when Edward
"goest forth and art anointed King," Watson went on to depict
the coming of night and with it the more serious thoughts attending upon such an occasion. And uppermost in the poet's mind was
the ephemeral nature of all things, particularly the kingdoms of
this world. Always especially sensitive to signs of decadence and
decline, in his fifth stanza Watson reminded the English of the
roads to destruction:

> O doom of overlordships! to decay
> First at the heart, the eye scarce dimmed at all;
> Or perish of much cumber and array,
> The burdening robe of empire, and its pall;
> Or, of voluptuous hours the wanton prey,
> Die of the poisons that most sweetly slay;
> Or, from insensate height,
> With prodigies, with light
> Of trailing angers on the monstrous night,
> Magnificently fall. (II, 100)

Warning his fellow countrymen to be ever awake to the threat which the militant nations of Europe constantly posed, Watson concluded, as one would expect, with a plea for an England of high ideals and virtuous actions. England must not, he emphasized, let power slip from her in a time of much peril, nor must she, like so many modern nations,

> . . . yield up yet
> The generous dreams! but rather live to be
> Saluted in the hearts of men as she
> Of high and singular election, set
> Benignant on the mitigated sea;
> That greatly loving freedom loved to free,
> And was herself the bridal and embrace
> Of strength and conquering grace. (II, 101)

In his "Lines to Mr. James Bryce," Watson wrote: "The great achievement of the human mind/ Is the idea of Justice" (II, 89) —a thought which can be taken as the keynote of the poet's political poetry. It was in the name of Justice that he had written his "Ver Tenebrosum" sonnets back in 1885; it was his love of Justice that motivated him to risk his high reputation as a poet and to write *The Purple East* sonnets of 1895; and it was his determination that the principles of Justice would prevail that once again led him to oppose his country in war and to bear the stigma of being reviled as "pro-Boer" at the turn of the century. In perhaps the most perceptive and sympathetic appraisal ever written of Watson's political poetry, Gilbert Keith Chesterton in his review of the poet's *For England,* a collection of poems on the Boer War, depicted Watson as a democratic poet in the line of Milton and Wordsworth. What Chesterton found in common among these men was their concern with the dignity of man, their preoccupation with the serious problems confronting the human race. Contrasting Milton with the aristocrats of his day, Chesterton wrote that "if we want a gay and gross picture of the real turbulence of the real rabble of the seventeenth century, say in England, we go to some cavalier like Dekker or Wycherley. To John Milton, the republican, we go for something quite different. We go to the republican not for a comedy about man but for an epic about man. Of this great tradition of the union of a democratic policy with a classical style," Chesterton declared, "the great living representative in England is Mr. William Watson. And he stands alone." What Chesterton cherished in the political poetry of Watson was, as he phrased it, "the old and authentic voice of the England of Milton and Wordsworth." Sympathetic to the poet's political idealism, the critic went on to say that Mr. Watson "loves the idea of the maidenhood of nations; vague and mountainous ideas like liberty, and a kind of sorrowful justice." With admiration, Chesterton quoted these lines from the sonnet, "Force and Freedom":

> But the fierce mountain stream of liberty
> Not edicts and not hosts can long restrain,
> For this is of the heights and of the deeps.

And then he remarked: "That is the Miltonic and the Wordsworthian England. It may be we are listening to the last of the ancient poets of England." [24]

Chesterton, unlike many of his contemporaries, understood Watson's intentions: to be what the great traditional poets of the past had always been—a spokesman for the nation's highest ideals, the voice which sought to counterbalance the nation's practical self which was all too often governed by self-interest and expediency. But too many of Watson's readers did not understand his position enough to appreciate his efforts, as his poem entitled "On Being Styled 'Pro-Boer'" clearly indicates. Accepting harsh words and ignorant accusations with humility, Watson wrote: "Friend, call me what you will: no jot care I:/ I that shall stand for England till I die" (II, 86). Despite years of disappointment, the poet was able to answer his critic with yet another affirmation of faith in the goodness of his native land, that England

> . . . from whose side I have not swerved;
> The immortal England whom I, too, have served,
> Accounting her all living lands above,
> In Justice, and in Mercy, and in Love. (II, 86)

IV *The "Pro-Boer"*

Watson's poems dealing with the Boer War appeared on October 5, 1903, in a small volume entitled *For England: Poems Written during Estrangement.* In sympathy with those of the Liberal party, such as Lord Morley and Sir Henry Campbell-Bannerman, who felt that war with the Transvaal should be avoided, Watson, once the war had begun, blamed his country for what seemed to him blatant aggression and tyrannous action against a small but sovereign nation of people whose humble, quietly courageous life he sympathetically depicted in "The Enemy":

> Unskilled in Letters, and in Arts unversed;
> Ignorant of empire; bounded in their view
> By the lone billowing veldt, where they upgrew
> Amid great silences; a people nursed
> Apart—the far-sown seed of them that erst
> Not Alva's sword could tame: now, blindly hurled
> Against the march of the majestic world,
> They fight and die, with dauntless bosoms curst. (II, 60)

If, as one critic expressed it, Watson in *The Year of Shame* sadly lamented the failure of England and in his "Coronation Ode" sang the glory of England, in his Boer War poems he passionately denounced the wrongdoing of his country.[25]

When *For England* appeared, the Boer War had ended and most reviewers, especially after reading Watson's "Dedication," acquitted the poet of any taint of having been unpatriotic. And since most of what could be said about the Boer poems had already been said about the *Ver Tenebrosum* sonnets and about *The Year of Shame* poems, the reviews were—appropriately enough—usually slight. In his brief essay, "Politics and Poetry," Francis Thompson noticed that *For England* showed that Watson's hand had "not lost its skill," even if the volume as a whole was "less compact in excellence, with a larger proportion of unnotable work than his best previous efforts in this kind." [26] While most critics, as a matter of course, were like the reviewer for the *Athenaeum* in pointing out that in *For England,* as in the poet's other political volumes, Watson "steadily pursues the precedent of Wordsworth in constituting himself a kind of chorus on the political drama of the day," [27] several observed the differences between Watson and his most formidable rival, Rudyard Kipling.

As Chesterton pointed out, no two poets could be more unlike than these men, one so typically English in his insularity, his proper often pompous pose; the other so un-English in his cosmopolitanism, his flair for lower-class dialect and shocking subjects. Whereas Watson drew his inspiration from the great Classical tradition of English poets, Chesterton saw Kipling's techniques and interests as stemming largely from the school of French Naturalism.[28] As the critic for the *Contemporary Review* summed it up, "It would be difficult to find in the whole field of 'literary psychology' a more striking contrast than that afforded by Mr. Rudyard Kipling and Mr. William Watson in their respective volumes of verse, 'The Five Nations' and 'For England.' Inspired by the same political events, and produced in the same national environment," he remarked, "these two books are as opposed in sentiment, language, and mental outlook, as though their authors belonged to different worlds." [29]

To be sure, Watson's world was one which had nothing in common with Kipling's fast-paced, rugged, cosmopolitan milieu. And this difference was but another sign, like the increasingly controversial spirit of his poems, that Watson was out of step with the aims and interests of the post-Victorian world. Since the 1880's, he had been a leader in the fight to uphold the principles of the Classical tradition in English poetry and to preserve the ethical ideals of Victorianism; but, by 1900, his continuing struggle to maintain the kind of mid-Victorian world into which he had been born was clearly ineffectual. As a result the poet found himself constantly at odds with a nation which no longer shared his opinions, his sensibilities, or his literary ideals. As he looked back over the years of Victoria's reign and soberly contemplated the first

[142]

The Tragic Change

Edwardian years, the full consequences of the tragic change came upon him: "To follow Truth was yesterday/ To England's heart the surest way," he mused; "Follow her now, and thou shalt share/ An exile's fate, an exile's fare."

CHAPTER 7

The Muse in Exile

Verse—a light handful—verse again I bring;
Verse that perhaps had glowed with lustier hues
Amid more fostering air.
                —William Watson, "The Muse in Exile"

O N DECEMBER 16, 1904, John Lane published *The Poems of William Watson* in two volumes with an introduction by John Alfred Spender, the editor of the *Westminster Gazette*, in which Watson's august position as a man of letters was clearly indicated in the opening lines by Spender's cautiously worded apology for standing between "the public and a poet of Mr. Watson's eminence. . . ." The recent recipient of a Doctor of Laws degree from Aberdeen,[1] Watson was at the height of a literary career which of all England's living poets seemed most secure. Yet his last popular, widely acclaimed poem had already been written, and the causes for his spectacular decline and, to some extent, their effects were present. It is indeed ironic that his last great success, the "Coronation Ode," was a celebration of a new age in which Watson's poetic idiom would find no place. Witness, for example, Vivian de Sola Pinto's critical opinion that the "Ode," was, "in spite of its technical dexterity, . . . verse written in a dead language and in rhythms that bear no relation to those of contemporary English life." [2]

I *Watson's Decline*

As Chesterton pointed out in 1903, Watson was by then an anachronism, "a typical Englishman," insular and nationalistic, who cherished the ethical idealism and the serious vision of life which was alien to the lower classes who had secured for themselves a dominant position in the scheme of things. According to

Chesterton, Watson was "a national poet" in a period of over-civilization when luxurious living led to a demand for the last and only luxury, novelty.[3] His pessimism, his moral earnestness, his highly conscious and carefully wrought art no longer appealed to the tastes of an age which craved the novelty of Kipling's foreign scenes, his Southern climes, his colloquial language, his rollicking rhythms, and his unbounded optimism and lust for life. Further-more, Watson's loyalty to tradition made it difficult for him—even if he had desired—to change with the times and to develop a less rhetorical idiom more responsive to the needs of the new age. As one critic expressed it, Watson had "subjected a by no means powerful genius to a training and discipline" that had "brought him exquisite sureness of taste and deftness of technique"; but, even within the limits of the Classical tradition, he had "failed to develop real richness of nature or any novel or distinctive en-visagement of life. He is too much of a poetic sacerdotalist," con-cluded the critic; "his authenticity has been his ruin." [4]

Long before the turn of the century, Watson had been aware of his precarious position and had sensed the growing lack of inter-est in his art and ideas. A poet who needed a sympathetic public to ward off his fits of dejection and to spur his imagination, Wat-son's uneasiness lest England slight him and heed not his words led to increased depression and pessimism which resulted in feel-ings of alienation and mistrust. The poet's reaction to this un-happy reversal of fortune and his attitude toward the increas-ingly alien literary scene are rather interestingly reflected in his essay of 1904, "The State Discouragement of Literature." Obvi-ously written soon after the New Year's Honors list was published, Watson charged that "In the distribution of honorific rewards to those who are considered to have served their country, literature seems expressly singled out for a studied and conspicuous dis-paragement." [5] Always a bit paranoid, Watson decided that the English no longer had a proper esteem for literature and the lit-erary man. For this sorry state of affairs, he mainly blamed the government and its educational policies which, he claimed, en-couraged an indifferent attitude toward the nation's great literary heritage. Furthermore, he rebuked the professional critics of the day who, as he expressed it, "abandon the entrenchments, . . .

let in the barbarian enemy," and actually "fortify that very spirit of assertive, invasive, rampant illiteracy which has so little need of reinforcement."

Because of these inhospitable conditions, Watson indicated their effect upon the man of letters. In short, indifference and discrimination depressed him and lessened his ability to do his best work. For, as he remarked, poets "are fashioned in the main like other men, subject to elation or depression from causes that similarly affect their fellows, and with the same perfectly legitimate desire for the things that give an outward dignity to life." In the highest realms of imagination and creative endeavor, "a genial spiritual climate is necessary to the full fruition of individual powers." [6]

That this essay reflected largely Watson's own plight is indicated in several letters he wrote to John Lane during the year of 1906. Suffering from a serious decline in poetic inspiration and a consequent inability to write, Watson told his publisher that he had reached a point where he simply could not write any more poetry. Like the Coleridge of the "Dejection Ode" who had lost his shaping power of the imagination, Watson seemed to think his springs of poetic creativity had run dry. Echoing the widespread Romantic notion that youth was the age of poetic inspiration, he confessed that he was now middle-aged and saw life "in a greyer light than the rosy mist through which it once was visible." As a result, he was through as a poet and longed for prose work of a critical nature. But even prose efforts, he made clear to Lane, required the promise of some definite monetary reward. Taxing Lane with the fact that he did nothing to help stop the steady drain on his capital, Watson demanded that the publisher make him some kind of lucrative offer which would enable him to leave poetry and to write a prose work which would sustain his fortunes both literary and monetary.[7]

That the poet wrote these words in all seriousness is indicated by another, even more extraordinary letter to Lane dated some six months later. Repeating the facts concerning his financial situation, Watson showed his irritation with the publisher for ignoring him and for appointing someone else as editor of his proposed independent review. Emphasizing his belief that he could only preserve his health if he did not write any more poetry, Watson explained again to Lane his need for some less imaginatively demanding occupation, such as editing a journal.[8]

There can be little doubt that Watson was, as time went on, finding it increasingly difficult and extremely distasteful to write poetry. Never overflowing with poetic inspiration, Watson now found the task of producing a poem almost excruciating and emotionally exhausting—a state which accounts in part for the fact that he had written but a handful of poems—only one of which, the "Coronation Ode" was of any worth—since *The Hope of the World* volume in 1897. Lunching with Churton Collins in April, 1907, Watson was asked why he was writing so little poetry. He replied, "because of the labour work costs me." [9]

Certainly Watson's failure to produce substantial volumes of verse at the turn of the century did much, as John Lane later observed, to undermine his eminent poetic position. While he was making but feeble efforts, poets like Kipling were attracting attention and winning the public's allegiance. Loss of inspiration, declining sales, rising competition, and public insensitivity to his traditional poetic mode were no doubt largely responsible for Watson's twelve lean years in which his literary position slipped noticeably. But John Lane also was correct in believing that the inheritance the poet received from his uncle's estate early in 1899 had helped destroy his incentive to produce poetry.[10]

Whatever the specific reasons for Watson's incredible plunge into oblivion as the new century went its way, Watson was, despite appearances, on his way down when the celebrated collected edition of his poetry was published in December, 1904. And, as his popularity declined and feelings of alienation and dissatisfaction increased, Watson became more and more preoccupied with the theme which he had announced in "England My Mother" and had elaborated in "The State Discouragement of Literature." Reviving a kind of crusade of the early 1890's once led by Walter Besant for public and state recognition of authors, Watson gained widespread attention in April, 1909, when he wrote a letter to the editor of the *Times* entitled "The Tragedy of John Davidson." Seeing Davidson's wretched death as but "one more addition to the long list of tragedies which we may consider as

beginning with the death of Spenser 'for lack of bread' . . . ,"
Watson dramatically declared that the poet's "blood is upon us, as
surely as if we had slain him with our very hands." [11]

II *The Asquith Affair*

If Watson's futile attempts to create within his fellow countrymen an adequate understanding and appreciation of the poet's
role in the national life reflected his own plight, the most sensational event of his life resulted from a poem which might be described as the objectification of the anger and frustration which
had been boiling within him for some time. Of the opinon that he
was no longer adequately appreciated and supported by his nation and its government, Watson focussed all of his suppressed
emotions upon Prime Minister Herbert Asquith, his wife "Margot,"
and his daughter Violet in the viciously satirical poem "The
Woman with the Serpent's Tongue." That Watson's bitter feelings
should have found their center in Asquith and his family is not
surprising, for the prime minister had led the imperialist faction
of the Liberal party during the Boer War while Watson had found
his ideal in Campbell-Bannerman who captained the "pro-Boers."
Naturally Watson was not at all happy later when Asquith succeeded Campbell-Bannerman as prime minister in April, 1907.
Furthermore, Asquith again angered Watson in the debate over
the state's treatment of literary men in the spring of 1909. Watson's coolness towards Asquith at this time is indicated by the fact
that the poet balked John Lane's efforts to obtain a knighthood
for him by excusing himself from receptions to which the prime
minister had invited him.[12] Finally, however, in June, 1909, Watson happened to meet Mrs. Asquith and Violet, her stepdaughter,
at Stafford House; and he accepted their invitation to tea on the
following Tuesday at 10 Downing Street.

At what turned out to be a fateful meeting for him, Watson
conversed with Violet for about an hour before Mrs. Asquith appeared. And it was during this time the daughter made what Watson took to be indecorous and insulting remarks about the recently dead Campbell-Bannerman. Watson left; and, as he
walked to the Devonshire Club where he was residing, he composed the quatrain "To the Memory of the Late Sir Henry

Campbell-Bannerman," which he sent to Violet with an offer to inscribe it in her manuscript book. Ignoring what Watson intended to be "an unforgiveable insult," Mrs. Asquith courteously replied to Watson's letter, and the affair was presumably over. However, Watson not only composed "The Woman with the Serpent's Tongue" but also soon after wrote an account of the tea at 10 Downing Street in order, as he later stated to reporters, "to explain the circumstances under which the poem was written and the incidents which inspired it." [13]

Then in the autumn he published the poem in various periodicals, including the New York *Times,* as well as in his volume of October entitled *New Poems.* The identity of "the woman" was scarcely in doubt for long, and in both England and America the poem became a favorite topic of conversation. Meanwhile, Watson, a bachelor of fifty-one, had married an attractive Irish girl, Maureen Pring, on August 11, 1909, after a whirlwind courtship of two weeks.[14] Late in November Watson and his wife boarded the *Lusitania* bound for New York. On their arrival on Friday, December 3, they were besieged by reporters who wanted to know if the woman with the serpent's tongue really was Margot Asquith and if he really intended to challenge Richard Le Gallienne (who was then living in New York) to a fist fight refereed by Tom Sharkey and Jack Johnson. Watson boldly faced his interrogators and denied, as he had done previously in a letter to John Lane, that he had any specific woman in mind when he wrote the poem. As to a bout with Le Gallienne (who had gotten into the act by writing a poem entitled, "The Poet with the Coward's Tongue"), Watson called it "all foolish talk. It is true that Le Gallienne and I are no longer friends, but—" [15]

Although "The Woman with the Serpent's Tongue" had already stirred up a controversy of considerable proportions, the most sensational events were yet to occur. For, after the other reporters had left his stateroom, Watson gave a reporter for the New York *Times* the account of his conversation with Violet Asquith which he had had typed the previous June. As a result, on Saturday morning, December 4, at the top of the front page of the paper were the headlines: "Watson Names the Asquiths." Immediately below was a transcript of a signed statement by Watson asserting that

The Woman with the Serpent's Tongue is a composite photograph of Mrs. Asquith and her stepdaughter Violet. The poem is a portrait of the physical characteristics of Mrs. Asquith and the mentality of Violet Asquith. The latter is the voice of the family and rules them all. Violet is the real official voice speaking with authority. She it is

> Who slights the worthiest in the land,
> Sneers at the just, contemns the brave,
> And blackens goodness in its grave.

Within a matter of hours newspapers in New York carried the spectacular revelation and overnight Watson's name was infamous. Outraged by the poet's ungentlemanly attack upon the respectability of two such eminent women, the public registered such a thunderous protest that Watson and his wife were all but driven instantly from the country.[16] On Monday, December 6, the *Evening Mail* headlined the charge by a leading New York minister, the Reverend Dr. Charles F. Aked, that Watson was either a cad or insane. And, after considering Watson's account of his June meeting with the Asquiths, the New York *Times* was of the opinion that "There seems to be no excuse for the existence of the poem ["The Woman with the Serpent's Tongue"], thus explained, except the temperamental irritability, the distorted vision, and the childlike inexperience of the poet." [17]

No sooner had the outcry against Watson begun to subside than the poet's brother, Robinson, now living in Montreal, appeared in New York. He had been moved by the "caustic statements" of Dr. Aked to defend his brother and explain his deplorable actions. On December 18, the *Evening Mail* carried on its front page a large picture of the poet and a lead article entitled: "Brother of Watson Says He Is Insane." To say the least, another sensation was immediately provoked when Robinson's revelation reached the public. In an exclusive statement to the *Mail,* the brother said that Watson had "come to the United States with a 'mission of hostility' against the family of Premier Asquith, and that all the sensational implications in the now world-famous 'The Woman with the Serpent's Tongue' are the result of hallucinations in a disordered brain." [18] Recalling the poet's mental breakdown of 1892, Robinson appealed to the public for sympathy by assuring the readers that Watson, on his return to sanity, would "deplore and decry his own bitter accusations."

In order to escape from his brother and the chaos which had descended upon him, Watson took his wife and silently stole away to Havana, Cuba, where he vacationed until it was safe to return to New York. To be sure, the Asquith affair in the United States was soon forgotten, but such was not the case in Britain to which Watson returned only to be snubbed and ostracized by society. There can be little doubt that "The Woman with the Serpent's Tongue" was the final blow to Watson's declining fortunes.

The poem itself is a striking example of Watson's ability to create bitterly satirical portraits in verse—one comparable in its scathing invective to the early unpublished portrait of Hall Caine. In the poem's first stanza, Watson's "composite portrait" is quite evident:

> She is not old, she is not young,
> The Woman with the Serpent's Tongue,
> The haggard cheek, the hungering eye,
> The poisoned words that wildly fly,
> The famished face, the fevered hand,—
> Who slights the worthiest in the land,
> Sneers at the just, contemns the brave,
> And blackens goodness in its grave.

The volume in which it appeared, *New Poems,* was Watson's bid for a revival of interest in his work; but the presence of "The Woman with the Serpent's Tongue" destroyed any salutary effects the volume might have had. Besides the "Sonnets to Miranda" which were dedicated to Millicent, Duchess of Sutherland,[19] there was little else of worth to be found. "Indeed," as one reviewer remarked, "with a few exceptions, this is a padded volume of trifles. But the poem that stamps on a woman gives the volume distinction, and the drinking song ["Tavern Song"] is as jolly as Shakespeare." [20]

The following year Watson again found Edward VII the subject of his poetry. In the title poem of the volume *Sable and Purple with Other Poems,* published in June, 1910, Watson mourned the death of a monarch who had served his nation surprisingly well and in doing so had gained its devotion and gratitude. "Born with a nature that demanded joy," Edward had taken, as Watson expressed it,

> . . . full draughts of life, nor did the vintage cloy;
> But when she passed from vision, who so long
> Had sat aloft—alone—
> On the steep heights of an Imperial throne,
> Then rose he large and strong,
> Then spake his voice with new and grander tone,
> Then, called to rule the State
> Which he had only served,
> He saw clear Duty plain, nor from that highway swerved,
> And, unappalled by his majestic fate,
> Pretended not to greatness, yet was great.

After the *Sable and Purple* volume, Watson tried his hand at drama, perhaps in an effort to regain his once exalted literary position by showing renewed creative vigor and literary versatility in a distinguished poetic mode. He returned to the manuscript of a play entitled *Phantasmopol* which he had been hard at work on in the summer of 1897.[21] Reflecting his preoccupation at the time with political subject-matter and the theme of justice, Watson's play was, as one critic expressed it, a "protest against tyranny, injustice, and militarism—a proclamation of the final triumph of good over evil." Published as *The Heralds of the Dawn* in May, 1912, the blank-verse play attempted to dramatize the coming of a new age of justice and liberty to the nation, Ideonia, which had been the victim of a king with an Old-Testament notion of God and of a brutal military leader devoid of moral character. Like Aeschylus' Apollo in the *Eumenides,* the handsome prince Hesperus is the spokesman for a more humane concept of law and for a higher idea of deity. Pleading with his father to show mercy to Abbo of the Woods who has murdered the victorious general of the army, Volmar, because he had violated his daughter and caused her death, Hesperus declares:

> God is more just than thou dost picture Him.
> Dost thou suppose He is a bartering God,

> That makes a profit out of our poor folly,
> Alert to seize on our unwariness,
> To catch us tripping and stickle for a price?

Although Watson had written the play "with a distinct view to theatrical production," [22] it lacked the vitality and the full-bodied characterization needed for stage success. In the opinion of the spokesman for the *Yale Review*, Watson's heralds were "strangely ineffectual; shadows of shades, abstract literary types who neither stir our feelings nor trouble our dreams." Discussing the plays of August Strindberg and Galsworthy's *The Pigeon* along with Watson's drama, the critic was struck by the abstract quality of *The Heralds* which seemed to him "to withdraw it from all contact with the spirit and temper of our age." [23]

III *Second Visit to America*

After a second trip to America in 1912 when he lectured in various cities and colleges, including Princeton and Yale, Watson published *The Muse in Exile* in April, 1913, which included a speech entitled "The Poet's Place in the Scheme of Life." In this address to Americans, Watson carried on his crusade for an intellectually enlivened public appreciative of the poet's role in life. Of the opinion that society's indifference to the poet was a phenomenon of the modern world, Watson inquired into the causes of this condition. Rejecting the notions that the age was too busy and fast-paced to bother with poetry, and that science, the great competitor of *belles lettres*, had supplanted it, Watson, in a critique of modern criticism, held its practitioners responsible for the indifference of the reading public. Reiterating what he had said in connection with this matter in "The State Discouragement of Literature," the poet described the various types of perverse critics from the one "who finds it pays him to have a bee in his bonnet, since brilliantly unsound criticism is often more readable than criticism which is unbrilliantly sound," to the critic "who is eternally demanding that poetry should be progressive, and to whom progress means a kicking against tradition and a violent breach with the past." One of Watson's major points was "that the total effect produced upon the 'reading public' by this orgy of critical individualism is a distracting and bewildering one, and that it makes seriously against the appreciation of what is good in contemporary poetry."

Reminiscent of his quarrels with the novelists in his early critical essays, Watson's assertion that "Fiction is really the archenemy of literature at the present time," clearly indicates the poet's attitude toward the form of literature which had supplanted poetry in the hearts of the public. Admitting that the novel in the hands of the very greatest masters could truly be considered great art, Watson pointed out that in lesser hands the form degenerated into a mere game "of keeping up the ball of the narrative, of holding the reader's attention by alternately gratifying and piquing his curiosity, of resorting to innumerable shifts and transparent devices which are scarcely the methods of art, in the great sense of that word."

Having described the plight as well as the enemies of the poet, Watson went on to suggest a remedy. "If you wish your poets to blossom and fructify as Nature may have intended," he asserted, "you must give them some warmth and sunshine." Declaring that the "true function of the poet today is to keep fresh within us our often flagging sense of life's greatness and grandeur," he urged his audience to appreciate and enjoy that service. But do not ask the poet to sing in solitude, he rather touchingly reiterated: "Do not ask him to sing before an audience which visibly melts away while he sings. Give him something of your hearts, and he will give you all his own heart in return. Give him a place—an honourable and honoured place—in your scheme of life."

Versifying his belief that the poet born in the later nineteenth century grew up "in an Arctic environment of perpetual frost," Watson in the title poem, "The Muse in Exile," painted a most dismal picture of the poet's predicament in the modern world. Describing the twentieth century as "an Age/ That banishes the poets" and

> . . . drives them coldly forth
> From where alone they yearn to live—her heart;
> Scourges them with the scourge of apathy,
> From out her bosom's rich metropolis,

[154]

The Muse in Exile

> To a distant, desert province of her thoughts,
> A region grey and pale: . . .

Watson concluded with a prediction that someday man shall once more feel the need of song "and call the exile home."

Another outgrowth of Watson's American tour found in *The Muse in Exile* is "The Centenary of Dickens," a poem which he read at the hundredth anniversary celebration of the novelist's birth held at Carnegie Hall on the evening of February 7, 1912.[24] Although his opinion of the novel was not high, Watson glowing tribute leaves no doubt that he considered Dickens one of the "very greatest masters" of that art form. Describing Dickens as a fighter who "did not fight to rend the world apart," but "fought to make it one in mind and heart," the poet rejoiced that

> . . . still, across the years,
> His soul goes forth to battle, and in the face
> Of whatsoe'er is false, or cruel, or base,
> He hurls his gage, and leaps among the spears,
> Being armed with pity and love, and scorn divine,
> Immortal laughter, and immortal tears.

The critics did not receive *The Muse in Exile* with much compassion or with much enthusiasm. The "undercurrent of pessimism" ruined the effectiveness of the volume for the New York *Times* reviewer, and the critic for the *Literary Digest* described as "unfortunate" Watson's "uncomplimentary" and "erroneous" opinion of his age.[25] An interesting illustration of the reception Watson's *Muse* received in the more *avant garde* periodicals are the two references to the volume in the little magazine, the *Blue Review*. Taking exception to the poet's evaluation of the novel, J. D. Beresford labelled Watson's statements about Dickens as "absurd, a mere sentimental trifling with ideas." And Lascelles Abercrombie in the same issue snapped, "Of Mr. Watson's 'The Muse in Exile' . . . I will not say anything at all; I have too much respect for Mr. Watson's past." [26]

IV Pencraft

Long irked by the desire on the part of an increasing number of men of literature to free their work from the heightened language and rhetorical devices which had come to be a mark of "literature," Watson deplored their attempts to shape poetry along the lines of the so-called language of the streets. Unable to understand so perverse an attitude toward the literary language of tradition, he made this modern phenomenon the focal point of his prose work entitled *Pencraft, a Plea for the Older Ways* which John Lane published in November, 1916. Trying his hand at something of a critical nature, as he had earlier proposed to do, Watson divided literature into three kinds: cantative, scriptive, and loquitive.[27] He was primarily interested, however, in the scriptive category because it embraced that "immense middle region that is absolutely literature; neither a sublimely abnormal, half preternatural phenomenon nor a transfiguration of everyday chit-chat, but absolutely literature. And," he went on to say, "this immense middle region has a distinctive language of its own, a language which is neither the language of gods nor of *gamins,* but just the language of literature" (18).

This language of literature, what he referred to as "pencraft," Watson sought to defend against the hosts of literary men who had turned traitor to their own peculiar voice and had adopted the most ineffective, imperfect form of speech, "the language of real life," as their preferred mode of expression. Contending that the literary language of tradition represented the successful attempts of man to develop slowly but surely "a form and mode of human speech" which was freed "from all the ten thousand hampering accidents which nullify and paralyse the language of real life whenever it essays to perform any of the nobler offices of expression" (20), Watson, in his most comprehensive and carefully considered attack upon those "who positively and openly resent sound workmanship and high finish," noticed that this tendency toward rough verse and colloquial language was but a manifestation of a recurrence "in our literature of something disordered and disorderly" (29–30).

It is obvious throughout the essay—just as it was in his critical essays of the late 1880's—that Watson had the born prose writer's attitude toward poetry: that verse, like prose, should be primarily a mode of logical expression. Neither the cantative nor the loquitive were controlled and shaped enough by the rational processes to satisfy his deep-seated need for carefully articulated ideas

fashioned into finely wrought forms. Almost always an unimpassioned, consummate artist in verse, Watson could never understand that poetry was most clearly and distinctly poetry when it
—by way of "illogical" means such as symbol, ambiguities,
metaphor—conveyed emotions and experiences which never
could be expressed in logical terms in prose. Why, he kept asking,
with all the consummate means man has developed to express
logically his thoughts and emotions, do poets periodically resort
to what for him were obscure and uncouth modes of language.

In this very matter his discussion of Browning's "Andrea del
Sarto" is very revealing. Referring to the central doctrine of the
poem as "the great modern heresy in criticism" (74), Watson admired Andrea's art but abhorred his perception that "less is more."
Unable to see what Browning and his Andrea saw—that though
technically imperfect, Raphael's work conveyed emotions and
insights that Andrea's flawless work could never express—Watson thought the central lines of the poem "hopelessly confused"
(78) simply because he himself was constitutionally unable to accept the fact that man's deepest emotions and highest perceptions
could not be fully expressed in terms of what the rational intellect deems perfect form and lucid statement. In fact, this very
inability to see that the "spirit"—that which Andrea called the
"light of God"—could not be expressed by rhetorical means kept
Watson from ever being a poet in the true sense of the word:
one, that is, who can on occasion convey in words intuitions and
spiritual intimations which lie beyond the rational powers of
man to express. Consequently, he never succeeded in anything
but a kind of poetry of statement which is closer to prose—what
he himself described as "pencraft"—than to poetry. Convinced—
as he abundantly made clear in his essay—that poetry was noble
thoughts and sincere emotions allied to technical perfection, Watson never once thought of extending the meaning of "technical
perfection" to the poet's use of whatever language resources were
available so long as they fully expressed his passions and insights.
In *Pencraft* Watson pleaded for a renewed respect for a literary
language which in its exactness and felicity of expression transcended all the verbal ugliness, the ineptness, and the mutability
to which the language of everyday life was heir.

Remarking that Watson of late had "been making poetry a

criticism of art rather than a criticism of life," a reviewer of Watson's *Retrogression and Other Poems*, the second volume of 1916, noticed that many of the new poems were hardly more than "versifications of passages in his 'Pencraft.' " [28] How true this observation was is immediately evident upon reading the first and title poem of the volume which advises those who have in them "Aught thou canst better sing than say" to

> Shun, if thou wouldst by men be heard,
> The comely phrase, the well born word,
> And use, as for their ears more meet,
> The loose-lipped lingo of the street,
> A language Milton's kin have long
> Accounted good enough for song.

Belaboring the same observations he had made in previous poems and prefaces, Watson in "Retrogression" continued to mourn the prevalence of "the unplenished brain!" and "The leanness of the unnourished mind." And in another tireless assault upon poetry made "Ragged and jagged by intent," he sought to prove that perfection of form in art was "Nature's Way": "Nature!" he exclaimed,

> . . . whose lapidary seas
> Labour a pebble without ease,
> Till they unto perfection bring
> That miracle of polishing; . . .

Of the opinion that "Nature's Way" as well as "much else" in the book was "sound in thought and brilliant in phrase," Odell Shepard in his review of *Retrogression and Other Poems* observed what was becoming abundantly clear: Watson had come "to enjoy thinking of himself as a sort of 'lonely antagonist of destiny,' a last survivor of the giants before the flood. It is a pity," this critic remarked, "that this mood of haughty isolation has grown so strong in his work of late." Referring to such poems as "To a Strenuous Critic," "The Yapping Cur," and "Coke Upon Littleton," Shepard observed that "The man who had successfully challenged Keats in 'Ode to autumn' and Arnold in 'Wordsworth's grave' and Milton himself in 'Lachrymae musarum,' might well afford to let alone all really ignorant or merely spiteful criticism of his work." [29]

In complete sympathy with his country during World War I, Watson gathered his poems dealing with that grim struggle together in a book entitled *The Man Who Saw and Other Poems Arising Out of the War.* Not unlike a diary, the volume is a record of the author's responses to the major occurrences beginning with a sonnet on "The Fourth of August, 1914" and concluding with "The Kaiser's Dirge" and several recruiting verses. Of interest in particular is Watson's sonnet "To the United States" in which he urged that nation's entrance into the war.

This volume also included several tributes to distinguished persons such as the sonnet, "The Three Alfreds," in which Watson praised King Alfred; Alfred, Lord Tennyson (whom he referred to as "Victoria's golden warbler"); and Alfred, Lord Northcliffe. Expressing his great admiration for David Lloyd-George, the wartime prime minister, Watson, in the title poem, "The Man Who Saw," depicted the Welshman as

> . . . a man
> Who in a time terrifically real
> Is real as the time; formed for the time;
> Not much beholden to the munificent Past,
> In mind or spirit, but frankly of this hour;
> No faggot of perfections, angel or saint,
> Created faultless and intolerable;
> No meeting-place of all the heavenlinesses;
> But eminently a man to stir and spur
> Men, to afflict them with benign alarm,
> Harass their sluggish and uneager blood,
> Till, like himself, they are hungry for the goal;
> A man with something of the cragginess
> Of his own mountains, something of the force
> That goads to their loud leap the mountain streams.

It was this tribute which probably gained for Watson the knighthood he had so long coveted. Lord Beaverbrook in *The Decline and Fall of Lloyd George* reports that Lord Stamfordham criticized knighting Watson because he had written "The Woman with the Serpent's Tongue." But "Lloyd George insisted upon keeping the name on the list because he said Watson had written *The Man Who Saw.*" [30] However it happened, Watson became Sir William on June 4, 1917, at which time the Civil List pension of one hundred pounds awarded in 1895 was doubled. Coming late as it did, the knighthood hardly carried with it the distinction it once bestowed, for by 1917 knighthoods were not held in much esteem by the English. At the time, it was not at all unusual for a man of distinction to decline the honor. In a remark which showed little respect either for the institution or for Watson, Richard Le Gallienne in a reference to the poet in *The Romantic 90's* equipped: "And, by the way, I should have said *Sir* William Watson, for most of my early friends seem to have become knights. Who was it, by the way, who said that 'London is now a City of Dreadful Knights'?" [31]

V *"The Superhuman Antagonists"*

After the strenuous and troubled war years, Watson found peace and contentment living, as he once wrote, "mainly among the majestic English mountains, partly on the lovely Irish coast, with my young children growing beside me . . ." And like the early years of his career when he wrote his fairy romance, *The Prince's Quest*, the poet found himself "once more dwelling in an atmosphere of romantic idealism akin to optimistic faith." [32] Out of this atmosphere of momentary calm came what Watson called his brief epic, the long poem in decasyllabic couplets, "The Superhuman Antagonists," which was based upon "the idea of a world ruled by two mutually hostile beings, Ormazd and Ahriman, the Good and the Evil Spirit" of Persian mythology (p. v). Like Milton's brief epic, *Paradise Regained*, the poem is a crucial confrontation in which the power for good, Ormazd, first realizes his power to overcome Ahriman, the source of evil. Miltonic in its cosmic setting; its heightened, rhetorical language and syntax; and in its characterizations, "The Superhuman Antagonists" (in later editions renamed "Ormazd and Ahriman, a Cosmic Romance") is a poem of slight plot in which an optimistic meliorism is espoused.

Published in September, 1919, *The Superhuman Antagonists and Other Poems* also contained a poem in iambic hexameters, "The Unreconciled," in which Watson lamented Ireland's refusal to wholeheartedly enter World War I. Always attentive to the plight of Ireland even before his marriage to one of Eire's daughters, Watson's idyllic mood in which he apparently wrote "The Superhuman Antagonists" was destroyed by his absorption once again in the cause of a victim of tyranny, Ireland. Hopeful in earlier years that the Irish nation might be reconciled to the Empire,[33] Watson by 1921 was dedicated to the complete independence of Ireland. In that year the poet published a volume of verse, *Ireland Unfreed*, and a prose pamphlet, *Ireland Arisen*, in behalf of Eire's independence. In much the same form, tone, and diction of his earlier political poems, Watson upbraided his nation in verses such as "Reprisal by Fire" and "Wasted Blandishments"; and he sang also the praises of Ireland's courage and righteousness in "The Bound One" and in "A Glorious Immunity." As Watson himself remarked in the Foreword to *Ireland Arisen*, the critical reception of *Ireland Unfreed* "wavered between wrath and scorn. Almost the least withering of their comments was— 'Rhetoric'!"

Toward the end of 1925 Watson published his last volume of new poems; and, although he was to live on for ten more years, oblivion had all but overtaken him. Suffering from respiratory ailments and heart trouble, Watson composed his *Brief Poems and New* in a nation and in a literary milieu in which he was literally an exile.

VI *The Last Years*

Watson's bitter, irreconcilable attitude of mind is strikingly revealed in the letters of his last ten or twelve years, one of the most extraordinary of which was written in response to a New Year's greeting on December 30, 1923. "There is a noble ring about the hope you express that 'every wish' of one's heart may be fulfilled in the coming year," he wrote his correspondent:

But you forget that this is quite impossible and unthinkable in the evil days on which I have fallen. Let me bring to your notice a fact or two. When I married, in 1909, I also published a book—"New Poems." My publisher advanced me £ 250 "on account" of royalties. Nothing further accrued from it, but what I want to point out is the following. I have subsequently published *eight other new books,* through five different publishing firms (Jenkins, Lane, Nash, Murray, & Hodder) *and from all those eight books put together* I have received less than the sum above mentioned, £ 250!!! In the 'nineties my vols. of poetry brought me about £ 500 a year. *They do not now bring me that sum in twenty years.* . . . May I ask you to bear these dreadful facts in mind if at any time you are disposed to think me a little ungenerous towards my 'Georgian' contemporaries—the men who, by something like an organised conspiracy against me (partly a conspiracy of depreciation & partly a conspiracy of silence) have pulled me down from former prosperity to miserable poverty, . . .[34]

And channelling his disappointment through the symbolism of poetry, he wrote:

> The Summer that begrudged its honey,
> And promised boons it never gave,
> Now, in its lean, mean parsimony,
> Departs unto its dirgeless grave.
>
> Come, honest Winter! Thou at least
> Wilt not thy lack of heart conceal,
> Or bid me to a monarch's feast
> To mock me with a beggar's meal.
> ("The False Summer," *Brief Poems and New*)

Although little remained of his once devoted, enthusiastic public, Watson even at the end had his devotees, as several reviews of his *Selected Poems* of 1928 reveal. In "Watson at Seventy," Robert U. Johnson, in the *Saturday Review of Literature,* declared without reservation that "This collection deepens the conviction that artistically Watson stands at the head of contemporary English poets."[35] And Wallace B. Nichols in the *Bookman* came to a similar conclusion after having attempted to convince his readers of Watson's ability to use the traditional literary resources creatively. Sir William Watson, he asserted, "not by virtue of merely being loyal to tradition, but because he has legitimately extended that tradition, stands at the head of the English poets living to-day."[36]

But Watson's few loyal admirers were hardly enough to wrest his fortune from the hands of those who saw his poetry as the last vestige of a rhetoric-ridden Victorianism which had long since ceased to speak with a living voice. Sinking ever deeper into poverty and obscurity, Watson's last years were—despite the love and devotion of his wife and daughters—a miserable existence almost unrelieved by any ray of hope. So serious were his straitened circumstances by 1930 that an appeal was issued for contributions to a testimonial fund for the poet who, read the announcement, "has remained loyal to the high purposes with which he set out, and has splendidly fulfilled them. . . . As a lord of language," it continued, Sir William "is in the Miltonic tradition. And now, after 72 years of life—58 years of it spent in the august but materially unremunerative service of his Muse—this oldest of our living poets lies ill and in poverty." [37]

Although the fund was a mark of esteem, as was his election in the same year to a corresponding membership in the American Academy of Arts and Letters,[38] Watson's fate had long been sealed. When his death occurred on August 12, 1935, many were shocked to learn that the poet had lived on for so many years.[39] Lacking the genius to create poetry of the highest kind, wholly dependent upon his extraordinary memory and its ability to combine in poems of "fancy" the echoes, images, and rhythms of the great poets of the Miltonic tradition, Watson had lost his vitality when that from which he derived his strength and inspiration failed to appeal to the mind and imagination of the modern world.[40] The voice preëminent of comfort and tradition to the last Victorians, Watson was in the twentieth century a poet in exile whose muse, indeed, had ceased to live.

Notes and References

Chapter One

1. See, for instance, Richard Le Gallienne, *The Romantic '90s;* Bernard Muddiman, *The Men of the Nineties;* Osbert Burdett, *The Beardsley Period;* and Holbrook Jackson, *The Eighteen-Nineties,* the most entertaining and rewarding of them all.
2. *The Classical Tradition in Poetry* (Cambridge, Mass., 1930), p. 7.
3. *Milton* (London, 1915), p. 220. See also p. 251 where Raleigh says Milton invented "poetic diction."
4. "An Agnostic Poet," *Sewanee Review,* VIII (July, 1900), 365.
5. "XII. The Springs of Helicon," *Collected Essays Papers &c. of Robert Bridges* (London, 1927–1936) (1933), II, 22. (I have taken the liberty of regularizing Bridges' unorthodox spelling in this passage.)
6. See James G. Nelson, *The Sublime Puritan: Milton and the Victorians* (Madison, 1963), esp. Chapter Seven, "Milton the Artist."
7. *Autobiographies* (London, 1955), p. 489.
8. William Butler Yeats, "Modern Poetry," *Essays by W. B. Yeats. 1931 to 1936* (Dublin, 1937), p. 10.
9. "Note on a New Poet," *Fortnightly Review,* LVI (August 1, 1891), 199.
10. Letter LXII, August 14, 1879, *The Letters of Gerard Manley Hopkins to Robert Bridges,* ed. Claude Colleer Abbott (London, 1935), p. 89. In this letter, Hopkins tells Bridges that he has cut himself "off from the use of *ere, o'er, wellnigh, what time, say not* (for *do not say*), because, though dignified, they neither belong to nor ever cd. arise from, or be the elevation of, ordinary modern speech."
11. "Introduction," *Oxford Book of Modern Verse: 1895–1935* (New York, 1937), p. ix.
12. Paul Marie Verlaine, "Art Poétique," *Oeuvres Poétiques Complètes* (Paris, 1959), p. 207.
13. *The Last Romantics* (London, [1949]), p. 211.
14. "Introduction," *Literary Essays of Ezra Pound* ([Norfolk, Conn., 1954]), p. xi.

15. *Literary Essays of Ezra Pound,* pp. 362–63.
16. G. Thomas Tanselle, "Two Early Letters of Ezra Pound," *American Literature,* XXXIV (March, 1962), 118.
17. "Introduction," *Oxford Book,* p. xii.
18. "Mr. William Watson's Poems," *The Speaker,* n.s. XI (14 January, 1905), 380.
19. "William Watson," *Poets of the Younger Generation* (London and New York, 1902), p. 517.
20. Laurie Magnus, "Mr. William Watson's Serious Verse," *Blackwood's Edinburgh Magazine,* CLVIII (July, 1895), 123.
21. Lawrence Churton Collins, *Life and Memoirs of John Churton Collins* (London and New York, 1912), p. 140.
22. G. K. Chesterton, "Watson's Poems," p. 380.
23. "Preface," *English Lyrics* by Alfred Austin, edited by William Watson (London and New York, 1890), p. xxiv.
24. Chesterson, *op. cit.,* p. 380.
25. J. Lewis May, *John Lane and the Nineties* (London [1936]), p. 96.

Chapter Two

1. *Correspondence of Thomas Gray,* 3 vols., ed. Paget Toynbee and Leonard Whibley (Oxford, 1935), III, 1109.
2. Lawrence Churton Collins, *Life and Memoirs of John Churton Collins* (London and New York, 1912), p. 252.
3. H. D. Traill [article actually written by William Watson], "The Passing Hour," *Black and White,* II (September 26, 1891), 419. Other sources of information about Watson's early life are: R. J. Lloyd, "William Watson," *Proceedings of the Literary and Philosophical Society of Liverpool,* no. LII (1897–98), pp. 2 ff.; "Mr. William Watson's Beginnings," *Daily Chronicle* (London), March 6, 1893 (probably but not certainly by James Ashcroft Noble); *Dictionary of National Biography,* 1931–1940. (London, 1949), pp. 893–94.
4. See Collins, *Life,* p. 253; Henry Bett, "The Poetry of Sir William Watson," *London Quarterly and Holborn Review,* CLXI (1936), 14.
5. William Watson, "Preface," *The Muse in Exile* (London, 1913), p. 8.
6. James Ashcroft Noble, "William Watson," *North Country Poets,* ed. William Andrews (London, 1888), p. 196. See also "Sir William Watson, the Poet," *Yorkshire Post,* April 25, 1930, p. 6.
7. William Watson, *Pencraft* (New York and London, 1916), p. 71.
8. "Preface," *The Muse in Exile,* p. 8.
9. "Mr. Davies, Mr. William Watson, and Mr. Ashcroft Noble,"

a letter to the Editor, *British Weekly*, XIII (December 22, 1892), 139.

10. *My Story* (New York, 1909), p. 52.

11. Collins, *Life*, p. 252. See also William Watson, "A Last Word on John Davidson," a letter to the Editor, *Times* (London), May 12, 1909), p. 8.

12. "A Personal Reminiscence," p. 154.

13. *My Story*, pp. 50–51; *Recollections of Rossetti* (London, etc., [1928]), p. 4.

14. Helen [Noble] Thomas, *World Without End* (New York and London, 1931), pp. 3–5.

15. *The Poems of William Watson*, 2 vols. (London and New York, 1905), I, 148–149. Future references to Watson's poems will be noted in parentheses in the text and will refer to this collected edition unless cited otherwise.

16. James Ashcroft Noble, "A Book of Beginnings," *Idler*, VII (1895), 248–55.

17. Liverpool *Argus*, October 21, 1876, p. 13.

18. Liverpool *Argus*, November 11, 1876, p. 60.

19. Rev. William C. Hall, "William Watson," *Papers of the Manchester Literary Club*, LXII (1937), 158–59.

20. Caine, *Recollections of Rossetti*, p. 4; Noble, "William Watson," p. 197.

21. Huntington Library MS: HM 1286.

22. "Ludwig Van Beethoven," *Graphic* (London), XV (March 31, 1877), 306, col. 2. This was Watson's first contribution to a London periodical, the first publication for which he received payment, and the first example of his criticism in verse.

23. Huntington Library MS: HM 22227.

24. See Watson's letter to the Editor, *Scottish Review*, typescript of original A.l.s. in Yale Library. Also see Collins, *Life*, pp. 252–53.

25. Review of *The Prince's Quest and Other Poems*, *Academy*, XVIII (August 28, 1880), 151.

26. Shelley's "Preface" to *Alastor*, *Complete Poetical Works of Shelley* (Boston, 1901), p. 33.

27. Review of *The Prince's Quest and Other Poems* [second edition, April, 1893], *Spectator*, LXX (May 20, 1893), 674–75. Probably but not certainly by Richard Holt Hutton. Watson in his conversation with Churton Collins reported in the text attributes the article to him.

28. Collins, *Life*, p. 254.

29. Coulson Kernahan, "Sir William Watson, an 'Old Contemptible' of Song," *Five More Famous Living Poets* (London, [1928]), pp. 283–85.

30. *Recollections of Dante Gabriel Rossetti* (Boston, 1898), p. 197.
31. *Sonnets of This Century* (London, 1886), in a note, p. 325.
32. *Academy,* XVIII (August 28, 1880), 151.
33. *Athenaeum,* no. 2756 (August 21, 1880), p. 237.
34. Huntington Library MS: HM 1276; reprinted in "Mr. William Watson's Beginnings" and in R. J. Lloyd, "William Watson." Watson's early poem is probably an imitation of Edward Dowden's "Seeking God" which appeared in *Poems* (1876).
35. *The Prince's Quest* (London, 1880), pp. 129–30.
36. Reported in J. Lewis May, *John Lane and the Nineties* (London, [1936]), p. 126.
37. Letter to the Editor, *Scottish Review,* November 1, 1907; typescript of original A.l.s. is in Yale Library.
38. See James Ashcroft Noble, "A Personal Reminiscence," p. 154; letter to the Editor, *Times,* December 15, 1892, p. 11, from James Bromley; New York *Times,* December 13, 1892, p. 2.
39. See Walter E. Swayze, "The Early Career of Sir William Watson, 1858–1905," Ph.D. dissertation in Yale Library, 1951, I, 66–67. Also see Lady Watson's unpublished life of her husband, *England Are You Proud,* Yale Library, pp. 30–31.
40. John Milton, "The Reason of Church Government," *Prose Selections,* ed. Merritt Y. Hughes (New York, [1947], p. 106.
41. "Areopagitica," *Prose Selections,* p. 259.
42. Collins, *Life,* pp. 254–55. Rossetti's advice to Watson in his letter of acknowledgment also may have influenced Watson's change of direction. In a letter to Hall Caine, Rossetti wrote: "I only wished him [Watson] to try his hand at clearer dramatic life. The dreamy romantic really hardly needs more than one vast Morris in a literature. . . ." Caine, *Recollections of Dante Gabriel Rossetti,* p. 197.
43. *Epigrams,* pp. 4–5.
44. *Ibid.,* p. 6.
45. W. B. Yeats, "A Scholar Poet," *Letters to the New Island* (Cambridge, Mass., 1934), pp. 206–7.
46. *Oxford Magazine,* II (May 7, 1884), 221–22.
47. *Academy,* XXV (March 1, 1884), 142.
48. "Ver Tenebrosum: Sonnets of March and April 1885," *National Review,* V (June, 1885), 484–89.
49. See R. C. K. Ensor, *England 1870–1914* (Oxford [1936]), pp. 77–84.
50. "What Is Public Opinion," *National Review,* V (July, 1885), 659.
51. Ensor, *op. cit.* p. 83.

52. "A Scholar Poet," *Letters,* pp. 207–8.

53. Adelene Wicks, "Mr. William Watson's Poems," *Matthew Arnold and the Spirit of the Age,* ed. Greenough White (New York, 1898), p. 140.

Chapter Three

1. Published in London by Elkin Mathews and John Lane, and in New York by Macmillan, March, 1893.

2. The six essays which represent a considerable undertaking begin in the January 6, 1877 issue of the *Argus* with a general article on music as an art form and continue in subsequent issues with essays on Bach and Handel. The anonymous essays were revealed as Watson's by James Ashcroft Noble in "A Personal Reminiscence," *Critic* [New York], n.s. XIX (March 11, 1893), 154.

3. *Academy,* XXV (June 21, 1884), 433.

4. A.l.s. in the Louise Chandler Moulton Papers, Library of Congress.

5. *Three Friends: Memoirs of Digby Mackworth Dolben, Richard Watson Dixon, Henry Bradley* (London, 1932), p. 139.

6. See Graham Hough's description of Eliot's *The Waste Land,* in *Image and Experience* (Lincoln, Neb. [1960]), esp. p. 22.

7. *English Lyrics* (London, 1890), p. xxiii.

8. "The Siege of Helicon," *National Review,* XIV (February, 1890), 826.

9. "Critics and Their Craft," *Excursions in Criticism,* p. 81.

10. *Ibid.,* p. 82.

11. Review of Walter's Pater's *Appreciations, Academy,* XXXVI (December 21, 1889), 399.

12. *Ibid.,* 400.

13. "Critics and Their Craft," *Excursions,* p. 85.

14. *Ibid.,* p. 84.

15. "The Fall of Fiction," *Fortnightly Review,* n.s. XLIV (September 1, 1888), 336.

16. "The Mystery of Style," *Excursions,* p. 105.

17. *Excursions,* p. 137.

18. "The Siege of Helicon," 828. This statement about "gropers" referred primarily to John Donne, the poetry of whom Emerson included in his anthology *Parnassus.*

19. "Dr. Johnson on Modern Poetry," *Excursions,* p. 152.

20. "Mr. Meredith's Poetry," *Excursions,* p. 137.

21. Preface to *English Lyrics,* p. xxiii.

22. "Dr. Johnson on Modern Poetry," *Excursions,* p. 598.

23. Preface, *English Lyrics,* p. xxiii.

24. *Excursions*, pp. 156–59.

25. Review of *The Shorter Poems of Robert Bridges, Academy,* XXXVIII (November 29, 1890), 496.

26. See in particular Watson's essay, "Lowell as a Critic," *Excursions,* pp. 89–96, and an unsigned review, "Mr. Lowell's Serious Poetry," *Spectator,* LXVII (August 22, 1891), 259.

27. "An Exposition of Walt Whitman," *Illustrated London News,* CI (July 9, 1892), 47.

28. *Ibid.*

29. "Ibsen's Prose Dramas," *Excursions,* pp. 129–30.

30. "Some Literary Idolatries," *Excursions,* p. 2.

31. Essay no. 4, Saturday, March 31, 1750, *The Rambler* in *Rasselas, Poems, and Selected Prose,* ed. Bertrand H. Bronson (New York [1952]), pp. 61, 62.

32. "'Coleridge's Supernaturalism," *Excursions,* pp. 98–99.

33. *Excursions,* p. 17.

34. "The Fall of Fiction," 324.

35. *Ibid.,* 325–27.

36. Dr. Johnson, *Rambler* Essay no. 4, *Rasselas . . . and Prose,* p. 60.

37. "The Fall of Fiction," 330.

38. *Contemporary Review,* LIV (October, 1888), 495.

39. *Fortnightly Review,* L, n.s. XLIV (November 1, 1888), 684, 688.

40. "Fiction—Plethoric and Anaemic," *National Review,* XIV (October, 1889), 168.

41. *Ibid.,* 169–70.

42. "Mr. Meredith's Poetry," *Excursions,* p. 138.

43. "Fiction—Plethoric and Anaemic," 171, 172.

44. *Ibid.,* 174, 180.

45. *Ibid.,* 183.

46. *Excursions,* p. 76.

47. *Excursions,* pp. 75, 78.

48. See Watson's reviews of Mary F. Robinson's [Madame Darmesteter] *Lyrics, Academy,* XXXIX (February 21, 1891), 179–80, and [Mrs.] Graham R. Tomson's *A Summer Night and Other Poems, Academy,* XLI (January 9, 1892), 30–31.

Chapter Four

1. *Poems of Sir William Watson, 1858–1935* (London [1936]), p. 283n.

2. This central section and Section IV which traces the course of poetry from Pope to Wordsworth do not appear in an early manuscript

version of the poem in the Huntington Library: HM 494. My references are to the text in the Collected Edition, I, 16 ff.

3. Review of *Wordworth's Grave and Other Poems, Academy,* XXXVII (February 22, 1890), 126.

4. *Autobiography of John Stuart Mill* (New York, 1924), pp. 103–4.

5. *The Autobiography of Alfred Austin, 1835–1910* (London, 1911), II, 218–19.

6. *National Review,* X (September, 1887), 40–45.

7. "William Watson," *North Country Poets,* ed. William Andrews (London, 1888), p. 197.

8. James Ashcroft Noble, "A Personal Reminiscence," *Critic,* n.s. XIX (March 11, 1893), 154. See also Grant Richards, *Memories of a Misspent Youth* (London, 1932), p. 150.

9. *Attitudes and Avowals* (New York and London, 1910), p. 190.

10. "Note On a New Poet," *Fortnightly Review,* LVI (August 1, 1891), 197.

11. *Letters to Edward Dowden and His Correspondents* (London and New York, 1914), p. 246.

12. *Letters to the New Island* (Cambridge, Mass., 1934), p. 205.

13. *Harper's New Monthly Magazine,* LXXXII (May, 1891), 968.

14. A.l.s. in Library of Congress. Mrs. Moulton remained one of Watson's staunchest partisans in America and lauded him in a essay on John Davidson in Stone and Kimball's *avant-garde* periodical, the *Chap-Book,* II (February 15, 1895), 291–92.

15. *Longman's Magazine,* XIX (November, 1891), 109.

16. Grant Richards, *Housman, 1897–1936* (New York, 1942), p. 340.

17. Hallam Tennyson, *Alfred Lord Tennyson, A Memoir by His Son,* II (New York, 1905), 392.

18. Review of *Poems, Academy,* XLI (March 12, 1892), 246.

19. *Spectator,* LXIV (March 8, 1890), 345.

20. *Letters to the New Island,* p. 205.

21. "William Watson," *Westminster Review,* CLX (November, 1903), 577.

22. "The Poetry of William Watson," *Sewanee Review,* III (February, 1895), 167

23. "William Watson," *Conservative Review,* I (May, 1899), 357.

24. That Watson was the author of several unsigned articles of 1891–1892 for the *Spectator* has recently come to light. See Robert H. Tener, "*The Spectator* Records, 1894–1897," *Victorian Newsletter,* XVII (Spring, 1960), 33–36.

25. A.l.s. in Library of Congress. Further references to this series of

Notes and References

letters are to the Louise Chandler Moulton Papers in the Library of Congress.

26. "Sir William Watson," *Five More Famous Living Poets* (London [1928]), pp. 291–92. For Robinson Watson's statement see *Evening Mail* [New York], December 18, 1909, pp. 1, 14.

27. Cf. Watson's lines with Shelley's "Adonais" in which he tells of Keats's spirit returning "to the burning fountain whence it came" and thus "He is made one with nature: there is heard/ His voice in all her music, from the moan/ Of thunder to the song of night's sweet bird."

28. For a thorough analysis of this poem, see Martha Hale Shackford, "*Shelley's Centenary,* by William Watson," *Studies of Certain Nineteenth Century Poets* (Natick, Mass. [1946]), esp. pp. 83–85.

29. "Dr. Johnson on Modern Poetry," *Excursions,* p. 150; see also "To Edward Dowden," where Watson spoke of Shelley as "somewhat lacking root in homely earth."

30. *Bookman,* II (August, 1892), 140, 142.

31. *Academy,* XLII (November 26, 1892), 476.

32. See typescripts, Yale Library, of letters from George H. Murray, Gladstone's secretary, to Grant Allen and Watson both dated November 17, 1892.

33. See typescript of Watson's letter to Edmund Gosse, postmarked November 22, 1892, Yale Library.

34. See Walter E. Swayze, "The Early Career of Sir William Watson, 1858–1905," Ph.D. thesis, Yale University, 1951, I, 312.

35. My statements concerning the period from Wednesday, December 7 through December 11, are based on the typescript of a letter from James Watson to Robinson Watson dated December 9, 1892, and typescripts of letters from A. C. Benson to Edmund Gosse dated December 9, 10, 12, 1892—all in Yale Library.

36. "Poet Watson in an Asylum," New York *Times,* Tuesday, December 13, 1892, p. 2; see also "Mr. William Watson," *British Weekly,* December 15, 1892, p. 119; and a letter from Watson's close friend, James Bromley, to the Editor of the London *Times,* Thursday, December 15, 1892, p. 11.

37. London *Times,* Wednesday, December 14, 1892, p. 9. A short report on Watson's health entitled, "William Watson," in New York *Critic,* n.s. XVIII (December 31, 1892), 369, began: "Mr. William Watson is still confined in the Roehampton Asylum, and shows, it is said, no signs of improvement."

38. "News Notes," *Bookman,* III (January 1893), 110.

39. "A Personal Reminiscence," p. 154. Noble also noticed that Watson's recent mental breakdown had evoked numerous references

"to a previous lapse from perfect mental balance; but those of Mr. Watson's friends who are familiar with the circumstances know that his former illness was largely due to a combination of causes to which the strongest might have succumbed. The cloud then passed speedily and completely, and every one will hope that the present cloud may not long remain."

40. "Mr. Davies, Mr. William Watson, and Mr. Ashcroft Noble," To the Editor of *British Weekly*, December 22, 1892, p. 139. Berry regretted the fact that Watson's "temporary debility should have been heralded to the world at large." But the unhappy facts did get abroad and rose up to blight Watson's life ever after. See for instance an inaccurate, irresponsible account of events which appeared in *Munsey's Magazine*, XIII (July, 1895), 343–44.

Chapter Five

1. *Spectator*, LXX (April 22, 1893), 522.

2. "News Notes," *Bookman*, IV (April, 1893), 5. See also a later note *re* Watson, *Bookman*, VII (November, 1894), 37.

3. The story which was published in *Macmillan's Magazine*, LXIX (March, 1894), 377–85, is the only fiction Watson wrote so far as I have been able to ascertain. Curiously enough, it is concerned with the mental breakdown of a beautiful young woman and exhibits considerable interest in neurotic and psychological ailments.

4. See "An Epistle" (I, 163), and earlier poems such as "The Questioner" (II, 210–11); "World-Strangeness" (I, 104); and "The Great Misgiving" (I, 119–20).

5. *Odes and Other Poems*, pp. 10–11. It is interesting to notice that Watson omitted these rather good stanzas from the revised version of the "Ode" found in the Collected Edition, I, 146.

6. "Mr. William Watson's New Poems," *Spectator*, LXXIII (December 8, 1894), 810–11; see also the review of *Odes and Other Poems*, *Academy*, XLVII (January 12, 1895), 28–29.

7. *Bookman*, VII (January, 1895), 114–15.

8. *Athenaeum*, CV (February 9, 1895), 177.

9. *Saturday Review*, LXXVIII (December 1, 1894), 603–4.

10. "William Watson," *Conservative Review*, I (May, 1899), 348.

11. Even before the death of Tennyson, the article, "Tennyson: and After?" appeared in the *Fortnightly Review*, n.s. XLVII (May 1, 1890), 621–37, and the author concluded, as did so many afterwards, that Swinburne was the only possible choice. Also the article forecast future sentiment when it suggested that, if Swinburne were not available, the laureateship should end.

Notes and References

12. Edward Valentine, "William Watson," *Conservative Review,* I (May, 1899), 348.

13. *Memories of a Misspent Youth* (London, 1932), p. 334. See also Watson's obituary, London *Times,* August 14, 1935, p. 7.

14. "Sir W. Watson's Poems," *Times Literary Supplement,* September 13, 1928.

15. Earl of Oxford and Asquith, *Fifty Years of British Parliament* (Boston, 1926), II, 248.

16. Richards, p. 151.

17. *Yellow Book,* V, 11–18.

18. *Bookman,* II, 182–83. See also "Who Should be Laureate?" *Idler,* VII (April, 1895), 400–19, in which nine literary figures (including Oscar Wilde, George Gissing, George Bernard Shaw, and John Davidson) told briefly whom they thought should be laureate.

19. *Bookman,* II (December, 1895), 292–97.

20. Oxford and Asquith, II, 248. For a full account of the laureate battle with particular emphasis on Alfred Austin, see Norton B. Crowell, *Alfred Austin: Victorian* (Albuquerque, 1953), esp. pp. 18, 20, 144. See also Owen Seaman's popular work, *The Battle of the Bays* (London and New York, 1896), esp. his parody of Watson, "Elegi Musarum," pp. 44–48.

21. See, for instance, P. H. Muir's article, "Elkin Mathews in the 'Nineties," *Book Collector,* I (Spring, 1952), 35.

22. *Paradise In Piccadilly, the Story of Albany* (London and New York [1925]), p. 106.

23. See J. Lewis May, *John Lane and the Nineties* (London [1936]), p. 208.

24. Reported in Kathryn Mix, *A Study in Yellow: the Yellow Book and Its Contributors* (Lawrence, Kansas, 1960), p. 149.

25. Reported in Furniss, pp. 113–14; also in May, pp. 209–10. In the mid 1890's Watson spent much time at the fashionable hotels in the Lake Country where he was seen spending holidays in the company of such notables as Lane, Aubrey Beardsley, and Max Beerbohm who predicted in a letter to a friend "a gushing friendship" with Watson. See Rupert Hart-Davis, ed. Max's *Letters to Reggie Turner* (London, 1964), p. 116.

26. Mix, p. 239. Also see *Friends of a Lifetime: Letters to Sydney Cockerell,* ed. Viola Meynell (London, 1940), p. 201.

27. May, p. 168.

28. May, p. 80.

29. May, p. 81.

30. For full accounts of the Beardsley affair, see Mix, esp. Chapter

XV, pp. 140–47; May, p. 80; J. Benjamin Townsend, " 'The Yellow Book,' " *Princeton University Library Chronicle* (Winter 1955), pp. 101–3; and Townsend's *John Davidson* (New Haven, 1961), pp. 182–183. See also note #21.

31. See, esp., John Lane, "Publisher's Note," *Under the Hill and Other Essays in Prose and Verse* by Aubrey Beardsley (London and New York, 1904), pp. viii-ix.

32. See, for instance, Watson's letter to the editor of the *Spectator*, entitled, "Wilde, and Whirling Words," LXVIII (March 26, 1892), 429. For Beardsley on Watson, see Douglas Ainslie, *Adventures Social and Literary* (London and New York, 1922), p. 225.

33. *Lachrymae Musarum*, pp. 48–49. The poem was not reprinted, for obvious reasons, in the Collected Edition. It first appeared in the *Spectator*, LXIX (July 9, 1892), 64.

34. Reported in Mix, p. 145.

35. *The Beardsley Period* (New York, 1925), p. 253.

36. "Mr. Watson's New Poem," *Spectator*, LXXIV (May 4, 1895), 607–8.

37. *Saturday Review*, LXXX (July 20, 1895), 71–73.

38. An exception to the statement is the review of *The Father of the Forest and Other Poems* in *Athenaeum*, No. 3553 (November 30, 1895), pp. 746–47, in which the author felt that the "Apologia" "read too much like a 'Letter to the Editor' turned into blank verse."

39. See "Mr. Watson's New Poems," *Spectator*, LXXV (November 16, 1895), 691–93; *Academy*, XLVIII (December 7, 1895), 479.

40. "Preface," *English Lyrics* by Alfred Austin (London and New York, 1896), p. xiii.

Chapter Six

1. Appeared in *Westminster Gazette*, December 16, 1895.

2. For a description of these events, see R. C. K. Ensor, *England 1870–1914* (Oxford, 1936), pp. 219–20; 238–39.

3. See also "To Mr. William Watson," *The Battle of the Bays* (London and New York, 1896), pp. 49–52, and Thomas Bailey Aldrich's "On Reading . . . Watson's 'The Purple East'," which appeared in the *Century*, LII, n.s. XXX (July, 1896), 374.

4. "Mr. Watson's Armenian Sonnets," *Spectator*, LXXVI (February 1, 1896), 169–71.

5. *Nation*, LXIII (October 8, 1896), 274. See also *Dial*, XXI (September 1, 1896), 120.

6. *Punch*, CX (February 15, 1896), 77.

7. *The Poets' Corner* (New York and London, 1904), plate #8. Reprinted in King Penguin Books (London and New York, 1943).

8. Richard Burton, review of *The Year of Shame, Bookman* (New York), V (April 1897), 165–66. See also William Morton Payne, *Dial,* XXIII (October 1, 1897), 188; Review of *The Year of Shame, Academy,* LI (January 9, 1897), 44.

9. Typescript in Yale Library of A.l.s. to Edmund Gosse, dated January 3, 1917, from Cambridge, England.

10. These lines which appeared in stanza vi of the original version of the poem in *The Hope of the World and Other Poems,* p. 6, were omitted from the version printed in the two-volume collected edition.

11. Watson originally wrote "The Dream of Man" in blank verse but later rewrote it in couplets without appreciably altering its meaning. As it originally stood, it was the most Miltonic poem in his entire canon. See the first draft (1891) in Yale Library.

12. The italicized lines are a paraphrase of Logion 5, lines 23–30 in ΛORIA IHCOY: *Sayings of Our Lord from Early Greek Papyrus* discovered and edited, with translation and commentary by Bernard P. Grenfell and Arthur S. Hunt (London [June] 1897), pp. 12–14. This work is the initial report of Grenfell and Hunt's findings at Oxyrhynchus in the Libyan desert south of Cairo which caused great consternation in religious circles in England. The best discussion of the collection of Logia is *Two Lectures on the 'Sayings of Jesus' Recently Discovered at Oxyrhynchus* by Rev. Walter Lock and Rev. William Sanday (Oxford, 1897).

13. See Lionel Stevenson's discussion of Watson's Darwinian concepts in *Darwin Among the Poets* (Chicago [1932]), esp. pp. 301–9.

14. *Yellow Book,* XII (January, 1897), 11–14.

15. See Watson's attitude toward the scientists' pride revealed in "Science and Nature," *Muse in Exile,* p. 94.

16. See Lafcadio Hearn's discussion of Watson's use of "the old Runic Measure" in "England My Mother" in "A Note on Watson's Poems," *Appreciations of Poetry* (New York, 1916), p. 352.

17. "Mr. William Watson's Poems," *Matthew Arnold and the Spirit of the Age,* ed. Greenough White (New York and London, 1898), pp. 137–38. Greenough White in "An Agnostic Poet," *Sewanee Review,* VIII (July, 1900), 377, remarked that Watson's "verse stores up the lost oozings of the Clough-Arnold tradition; . . ."

18. *Spectator,* LXXIX (September 4, 1897), 304–5. This is a review of "The Unknown God" which appeared in the *Fortnightly Review,* LXVIII, n.s. LXII (September, 1897), 321, 323.

19. Review of *The Hope of the World, Literature,* I (December 18, 1897), 259.

20. For John Lane's factual account of this affair, see the typescript at Yale Library of the original T.l.s.

21. A typescript of the original A.l.s. is in Yale Library. In a reply to Lady [Dorothy] Grey's letter of praise, Watson wrote: "It was very pleasant to receive your letter, both for its generous word about my ode and as evidence that my Liberal Imperialist friends have not all banished me utterly from their regard on account of my unfortunate opinions. (My sympathies are very apt to be with rebels, from Satan downwards.)" A.l.s. in the possession of the author.

22. *Academy*, LXIII (June 28, 1902), 7–8.

23. Sir Winston Churchill in "Freedom and Progress for All," *Listener*, XVII (May 5, 1937), 850, recalled these lines while discussing the almost miraculous formation and continued unity of the British Empire, and went on to remark that the famous admiral, Lord Fisher, used to recite Watson's lines to him before World War I. In "Baby Bunting," *Times* [London] (May 11, 1937), p. 17, the writer noticed that of all the coronation odes, only Watson's "caught on"; and in the lead editorial on Coronation Day, *Times* [London] (May 12, 1937), p. 13, the editorialist in "God Save King George" employed lines from the "Ode" as a basis for his comments.

24. "The Political Poetry of Mr. William Watson," *Fortnightly Review*, LXXX (November, 1903), 768.

25. W. Finnemore, "The Poetry of Sir William Watson," *Central Literary Magazine*, XXIV (April, 1920), 221.

26. *Academy*, LXV (October 10, 1903), 383.

27. *Athenaeum*, no. 3972 (December 12, 1903), p. 787.

28. "The Political Poetry of Mr. William Watson," *Fortnightly Review*, LXXX (November, 1903), 765–66.

29. *Contemporary Review*, LXXXIV (December, 1903), 904. See also Sir Arthur Quiller-Couch's review, *Bookman*, XXII (July, 1902), 130–31.

Chapter Seven

1. Watson received the degree April 6, 1904. See his poem, "To Aberdeen," II, 35.

2. *Crisis in English Poetry, 1880–1940* (London, 1951), p. 118.

3. "The Political Poetry of Mr. William Watson," *Fortnightly Review*, LXXX, n.s. LXXIV (November 2, 1903), 762–66.

4. Lewis E. Gates, "Three Lyrical Moods," *Studies and Appreciations* (New York, 1900), p. 174.

5. *Fortnightly Review*, LXXXI (February, 1904), 268–69.

6. *Ibid.*, 270–71.

7. Typescript in Yale Library of original A.l.s., dated January 21, 1906.

8. Typescript in Yale Library of A.l.s., dated July 3, 1906.

9. Reprinted in Lawrence C. Collins, *Life and Memoirs of John Churton Collins* (London and New York, 1912), p. 254. See also William C. Hall, "William Watson," *Papers of the Manchester Literary Club,* LXII (1937), 178, in which he mentions the fact that Watson had his workroom at Hawkshead covered with red paper. "What is the inference?" asked Hall. "Watson had come back to the Lakes for all the inspiration he could get, and had sought, among other things, the excitation of sheer colour."

10. See typescript of A.l.s. in Yale Library from Lane to Watson, dated January 21, 1910.

11. *Times,* April 26, 1909, p. 10. See also "A Last Word on John Davidson," *Times,* May 12, 1909, p. 8.

12. Lane with the aid of Augustine Birrell and James Bryce had evidently secured a knighthood for the poet in 1909; but Watson, failing to receive the customary letter of intimations, thought he had been passed over and, as Lane remarked, immediately began a campaign to blacken the name of the Asquiths. See typescript in Yale Library of A.l.s. from Lane to Watson, dated January 21, 1910.

13. The fullest, most accurate report of the Asquith controversy is the account in the New York *Times,* December 4, 1909, pp. 1–2, in which Watson's signed statement *re* the Asquiths and his account of the tea in Downing Street first appeared.

14. The wedding which was kept secret for several days was first announced in the *Daily Mail,* August 20, 1909: "It will come as a surprise to the literary world," the statement read, "that Mr. William Watson was privately married on August 11 at St. Luke's, Lyncombe, Bath, to a beautiful Irish girl, Miss Adeline Maureen Pring, of Howth, County Dublin." See Lady Watson's account of the courtship at Bath in her unpublished biography of her husband, *England Are You Proud,* in Yale Library, pp. 104–5.

15. New York *Evening Mail,* December 3, 1909, p. 4. In this early news account which appeared on the day Watson arrived in New York, the poet denied having the Asquiths in mind when he wrote "The Woman with the Serpent's Tongue." He had previously denied the fact in a letter to John Lane, dated October 31, 1909, typescript of which is in Yale Library. See Lady Watson's account of the trip to America and the Asquith affair in *England Are You Proud,* pp. 117–31.

16. See, for instance, New York *Sun,* December 5 and 9, 1909, pp. 10 and 5. New York *Times,* December 5, 1909, p. 1.

17. New York *Evening Mail,* December 6, 1909, p. 1; New York *Times,* December 5, 1909, p. 12.

18. New York *Evening Mail,* December 18, 1909, pp. 1, 14. Just what Robinson's motives were in coming to New York and releasing

such a statement to the press without his brother's permission is difficult to determine, but Watson accused his brother, from whom he had long been estranged, of leading "a conspiracy of which the object was to have me declared insane and treated as a lunatic.—that is to say, deprived of control over my own affairs, monetary and other; separated from the wife I had but lately wedded; and shut up in a madhouse in a foreign country." (See A.l.s. in Yale Library dated March 3, 1910, from Watson to the British Ambassador in Washington, the Right Honorable James Bryce.)

19. According to Sir Shane Leslie, Watson during the early summer of 1909 was "infatuated" with the Duchess whose famous literary parties at Stafford House were a mecca for artists and socialites. In a letter dated June 21, 1909, Watson told the duchess that he had composed a sonnet to her ("If you had lived in that more stately time," *New Poems*, pp. 23–24) but was afraid to inscribe it in the volume of verses he was sending her. When she requested the poem, he wrote an ecstatic reply in which he declared, "I send you the sonnet, with less of fear and trembling than were mine at first." (The two letters and the manuscript sonnet are in the possession of Sir Shane Leslie.)

20. *Independent*, LXVII (December 9, 1909), 1319. The critic in "A Static Poet," for the *Saturday Review*, CVIII, supplement (November 13, 1909), vi, called the poems "innutritious."

21. See Swayze, II, 487.

22. Watson in a letter in Yale Library to Richard Garnett, dated July 1, 1897, referred to the play when he wrote that he was spending the summer "hard at work on a drama, the subject of which is the freeing and regeneration of a people (an imaginary community). I am writing it with a distinct view to theatrical production, & to literary quality no less."

23. Lee Wilson Dodd, *Yale Review*, n.s. I (July, 1912), 690.

24. See New York *Times*, February 8, 1912, p. 2. Also of related interest are news items in New York *Times*, February 7, 1912, p. 7; the Magazine Section of the New York *Times*, February 11, p. 8; and New York *Times*, February 13, p. 10.

25. New York *Times Book Review*, XVIII (April 27, 1913), 253; *Literary Digest*, XLVI (April 26, 1913), 962.

26. "Anger and Dismay," *Blue Review*, I (June, 1913), 88; "Poetry," same issue, 121.

27. *Pencraft* (New York and London, 1916), p. 9. Further references to this work are cited in parentheses in the text. In a letter to Robert Ross dated November 24, 1916, Robert Graves, referring to *Pencraft*, wrote: "I'm sure Mr. Watson will be as pleased as myself

with that review—but W's book is not really seriously intended to convert Georgians to Victorianism is it? It's more or less an explanation of Vm, perhaps to help the Edwardian poets of thirty years hence in their reaction, but futile at the moment." *Robert Ross, Friend of Friends*, ed. Margery Ross (London, [1952]), p. 295.

28. *Literary Digest*, LIV (March 10, 1917), 633.

29. *Dial*, LXIII (June 28, 1917), 18.

30. *The Decline and Fall of Lloyd George* (New York, 1963), p. 25n.1.

31. *The Romantic 90s* (Garden City, N.Y., 1925), p. 2. See also Solomon Eagle [J. C. Squire], "Sir William Watson and Mr. Lloyd George," *Books in General* [1st series] (New York, 1919), pp. 254–58. For the official announcement of Watson's knighthood see *Times*, June 4, 1917, p. 10.

32. Preface, *The Superhuman Antagonists and Other Poems* (London, New York, Toronto [1919]), p. ix. Further references to this work will be cited in parentheses in text.

33. See, for instance, "England to Ireland" (written in 1888), "Ireland," and "The Three Neighbors."

34. Typescript in Yale Library of A.l.s. Also notice the attitude expressed, for instance, in a letter dated December 21, 1930, in which Watson denied a correspondent's assertion that he had been "buried" for years: "The thirty years of this century have been, in the main, years of strenuous work on my part, and some 14 or 15 volumes of verse and prose bear witness to it. These results may themselves have been 'buried', but the grave-digger has been a faithless public, aided by false friends and various inimical influences, public and personal, which I don't propose to discuss." (A.l.s. in Yale Library.) See also a letter to Richard Le Gallienne dated September 6, 1925, in which Watson wrote: "The tide of literary taste, at any rate in poetry, has as you know set very decidedly against me in this country. In fact the very atmosphere which made possible my years of success in the 'nineties has ceased to exist." As a result, Watson asked Le Gallienne (who was living in America) if he thought the atmosphere in the United States was similar to that in England, *"to such a degree* as to make it unlikely that I should have anything approaching to a warm welcome there, if I were to try my luck as a lecturer during the forthcoming winter?" (Typescript in Yale Library)

35. *Saturday Review*, V (August 11, 1928), 35.

36. "Sir William Watson," *Bookman*, LXXIV (August, 1928), 250. Nichols discusses Watson's use of free verse and various meters which he feels indicate ability to stay abreast of the times without breaking

with the literary past. Also see Ronald Campbell Macfie, "A Neglected Poet," London *Observer*, December 9, 1930.

37. "Sir William Watson," *Times*, November 3, 1930, p. 9.

38. Watson was elected an honorary corresponding member of the American Academy of Arts and Letters at the annual meeting November 13, 1930.

39. Watson died in a nursing home at Ditchling Common, Sussex, and was buried in Childwall Churchyard in Liverpool, August 16, 1935. His death received a surprising amount of attention in the press and is reported in the *Times*, August 14, 1935, p. 7 and in an editorial, p. 13. See also London *Observer*, August 18, 1935, p. 12.

40. For one of the most acute and penetrating critical appraisals of Watson ever written, see Lionel Johnson's critical sketch in Katharine Tynan, "A Catholic Poet," *Dublin Review*, CXLI (October, 1907), 336.

Selected Bibliography

BIBLIOGRAPHICAL DATA

There are three major collections of Watsoniana: the Sir William Watson Collection in the Library of Yale University; the Brotherton Collection in the Library of the University of Leeds; and the Walpole 'Nineties Collection in the Bodleian Library, Oxford University. There are also collections of Watson materials in the Huntington Library, San Marino, California; in the Library of Congress; and in the British Museum. See Walter E. Swayze, "The Sir William Watson Collection," *Yale University Library Gazette*, XXVII (1953), 71–76; "Sir Hugh Walpole's 'Nineties Collection," *Bodleian Library Record*, II (1942), 40–41.

Important check-lists of Watson's published volumes are: Cecil Woolf, "Some Uncollected Authors XII: Sir William Watson," *Book Collector*, V (Winter, 1956), 375–80; Norman Colbeck, "Some Uncollected Authors XII: Sir William Watson: Additions and Corrections," *Book Collector*, VI (Spring, 1957), 66–67; Walter E. Swayze, "Some Uncollected Authors XII: Sir William Watson: Additions and Corrections," *Book Collector*, VI (Autumn, 1957), 285–86, and VI (Winter, 1957), 402.

PRIMARY SOURCES

(Actual dates of publication are indicated in parentheses)

The Prince's Quest and Other Poems. London: C. Kegan Paul, 1880 (April).

Epigrams of Art, Life and Nature. Liverpool: Gilbert G. Walmsley, 1884 (January).

"Ver Tenebrosum: Sonnets of March and April, 1885," *National Review*, V (June, 1885), 484–89.

"The Fall of Fiction," *Fortnightly Review*, L (September, 1888), 324–36 [unsigned].

"Fiction—Plethoric and Anaemic," *National Review*, XIV (October, 1889), 167–83.

Wordsworth's Grave and Other Poems. London: T. Fisher Unwin (Cameo Series), 1890 (January).

"The Siege of Helicon," *National Review,* XIV (February, 1890), 826–34.

Poems. London and New York: Macmillan, 1892 (February 17).

Lachrymae Musarum and Other Poems. London and New York: Macmillan, 1892 (November 12).

The Poems of William Watson. New York and London: Macmillan, 1893 (January).

The Eloping Angels: A Caprice. London: Elkin Mathews and John Lane, 1893 (March).

Excursions in Criticism: Being Some Prose Recreations of a Rhymer. London: Elkin Mathews and John Lane; New York: Macmillan, 1893 (March).

Odes and Other Poems. New York and London: Macmillan, 1894 (November 30).

The Father of the Forest and Other Poems. Chicago: Stone and Kimball, 1895 (October 28); London: John Lane, 1895 (November 7).

The Purple East: A Series of Sonnets on England's Desertion of Armenia. London: John Lane, 1896 (January 24); Chicago: Stone and Kimball, 1896.

The Year of Shame. London and New York: John Lane, 1897 (December, 1896).

The Hope of the World and Other Poems. London and New York: John Lane, the Bodley Head, 1898 (December 4, 1897).

The Collected Poems of William Watson. London: John Lane, 1898 (December).

Ode on the Day of the Coronation of King Edward VII. London: John Lane, the Bodley Head, 1902 (June 13).

For England: Poems Written during Estrangement. London and New York: John Lane, the Bodley Head, 1903 (October 5).

The Poems of William Watson [ed. J. A. Spender]. 2 vols. London and New York: John Lane, the Bodley Head, 1905 (December 16, 1904).

New Poems. London: John Lane, the Bodley Head; New York: John Lane, 1909 (October).

Sable and Purple with Other Poems. London: Eveleigh Nash, 1910 (June); New York: John Lane, 1910.

The Heralds of the Dawn, a Play in Eight Scenes. New York and London: John Lane, 1912 (May).

Selected Bibliography

The Muse in Exile. London: Herbert Jenkins, 1913 (April); New York: John Lane, 1913.

Pencraft, a Plea for the Older Ways. New York: John Lane; London: John Lane, the Bodley Head, 1916 (November).

Retrogression and Other Poems. New York: John Lane; London: John Lane, the Bodley Head, 1917 (November, 1916).

The Man Who Saw and Other Poems Arising Out of the War. London: John Murray 1917 (May); New York and London: Harper and Brothers [June, 1917].

The Superhuman Antagonists and Other Poems. London, New York, Toronto: Hodder and Stoughton [September, 1919].

Ireland Unfreed: Poems and Verses Written in the Early Months of 1921. London: John Lane, the Bodley Head, 1921 (June).

Ireland Arisen. London: Grant Richards, 1921 (November).

A Hundred Poems. London, New York, Toronto: Hodder and Stoughton [November, 1922]; New York: Dodd Mead, 1923.

Poems Brief and New. London: Jonathan Cape [November, 1925].

Selected Poems. London: T. Butterworth, [June, 1928].

The Poems of Sir William Watson, 1878–1935. London, Bombay, Sydney: Harrap [July, 1936].

I Was an English Poet [compiled by Lady Watson]. Asheville, North Carolina: N.P., 1941.

SECONDARY SOURCES

ALLEN, GRANT. "Note on a New Poet," *Fortnightly Review*, LVI, n.s. L (August 1, 1891), 196–202. This article made Watson famous; praised him as a "True Blue" poet.

ARCHER, WILLIAM. *Poets of the Younger Generation.* London and New York: John Lane, 1902. An interesting critical estimate and survey of the poet's work at the turn of the century.

CHESTERTON, GILBERT K. "The Political Poetry of Mr. William Watson," *Fortnightly Review*, LXXX, n.s. LXXIV (November 2, 1903), 761–68. A very perceptive appraisal of Watson's political poems. Places Watson in the tradition of "democratic" poets such as Milton and Wordsworth.

FAIRCHILD, HOXIE NEALE. *Religious Trends in English Poetry, V: 1880–1920.* New York and London: Columbia University Press, 1962. In his discussion of Watson's poetry (pp. 21–26), Fairchild speaks of the poet as "a good nineteenth-century sentimental Liberal" who reluctantly worshipped an "Unknown God."

FIGGIS, DARRELL. *Studies and Appreciations.* London: J. M. Dent,

1912. The essay on Watson is an important discussion of the poems concerned with religion and agnosticism.

JOHNSON, ROBERT U. "Watson at Seventy," *Saturday Review of Literature*, V (August 11, 1928), 35–36. Claims that Watson is still at the head of contemporary English poets.

KERNAHAN, COULSON. "Sir William Watson," *Bookman*, LXIX (March, 1926), 291–95. A favorable, admiring review of Watson's poetry with pictures of Watson, his wife, and two daughters.

MAY, J. LEWIS. *John Lane and the Nineties*. London: John Lane [1936]. Contains important information concerning Watson's relations with Lane.

NICHOLS, WALLACE B. "Sir William Watson," *Bookman*, LXXIV (August, 1928), 249–50. Claims Watson extended the Classical tradition of English poetry by being metrically creative in later poems.

NOBLE, JAMES ASHCROFT. "A Personal Reminiscence," *Critic* [New York], n.s. XIX (March 11, 1893), 154. Contains important biographical facts about Watson's early years in Liverpool and important data on his early poetry.

PINTO, VIVIAN DE SOLA. *Crisis in English Poetry, 1880–1940*. London: Hutchinson's University Library, 1951. Sees Watson as "the typical poet of educated suburbia at the opening of the twentieth century."

STEVENSON, LIONEL. *Darwin Among the Poets*. Chicago: University of Chicago Press [1932]. Discusses Darwinian concepts in Watson's poetry.

SWAYZE, WALTER E. "The Early Career of Sir William Watson, 1858–1905." Ph.D. Thesis, Yale University, 1951. A carefully documented, detailed discussion of Watson's life and work to 1905. Contains an excellent bibliography.

TYNAN, KATHARINE. "A Catholic Poet," *Dublin Review*, CXLI (October, 1907), 327–44. Contains Lionel Johnson's superb critical appraisal of Watson.

VALENTINE, EDWARD A. U. "William Watson," *Conservative Review*, I (May, 1899), 347–61. A perceptive discussion of Watson's rise to fame and his status as one of England's leading poets at the turn of the century.

WATSON, LADY MAUREEN. *England Are You Proud*. [Unpublished biography of Sir William Watson in the Watson Collection in the Library of Yale University.] Lady Watson's reminiscences of her life with her husband.

WHITE, GREENOUGH. "An Agnostic Poet," *Sewanee Review*, VIII (July,

1900), 365–77. Presents Watson as latest in a Classical, agnostic tradition of poetry stemming from Clough and Arnold.

WOODBERRY, GEORGE E. "William Watson," *Century Magazine,* LXIV (September, 1902), 801–3. Asserts that in America Watson was the most widely accepted poet of the new generation at the turn of the century.

YEATS, WILLIAM BUTLER. *Letters to the New Island.* Cambridge, Mass.: Harvard University Press, 1934. The volume includes an interesting discussion of Watson's early poetry, especially *Epigrams of Art, Life, and Nature* and *Wordsworth's Grave.*

Index

Abercrombie, Lascelles, critical of Watson, 155

Aked, Charles F. (preacher), and Asquith controversy, 150

Allen, Grant (critic, poet, novelist), review of *Wordsworth's Grave*, 19; "Note on a New Poet," 77-78, 82, 84; mentioned, 107, 112, 113

American Academy of Arts and Letters, Watson elected corresponding member of, 163

Archer, William, on Watson and the Classical tradition, 23

Armenian controversy, Watson's poetry on, 117-23; Watson's depression as result of, 134-35

Arnold, Sir Edwin (poet), 108

Arnold, Matthew, influence on Watson, 53, 61-62, 125-28, 132; Watson's elegy on, 84-86; Watson's attitude toward, 85-86; mentioned, 16, 18, 61, 70, 79, 106; "Dover Beach," 132; *Empedocles on Etna*, 125-28

Asquith, Herbert (prime minister), Watson's dislike for, 148

Asquith, "Margot," subject of "The Woman with the Serpent's Tongue," 148-51

Asquith, Violet, subject of "The Woman with the Serpent's Tongue," 148-50

Austin, Alfred (poet laureate), publishes "Ver Tenebrosum," 50; opposes Watson's stand on Armenian question, 121-22; mentioned, 55, 76, 83, 108

Bach, J. S., Watson's essay on, 168n2

Baudelaire, Pierre Charles, influence on poets of 1890's, 20

Beardsley, Aubrey, dismissal from *Yellow Book*, 110-12; mentioned, 16, 18, 24, 25, 109

Beerbohm, Max, caricature of Watson by, 122-23; Watson's friendship with, 173n25; mentioned, 109

Benson, A. C., alarmed by Watson's visit, 95; Watson's poem to, 103

Bodley Head (publishing firm), partnership dissolved, 109; mentioned, 98. *See also* John Lane; Elkin Mathews

Boer War, Watson's poetry on, 141-143; mentioned, 15

Bridges, Robert, on Milton, 17; poetry praised by Watson, 60-61; mentioned, 19, 54, 69

Browning, Robert, Watson critical of, 55, 58-59, 68; aspiration in poetry of, 129; "Andrea del Sarto," 157

Bunyan, John, Watson's early reading of, 27

Burns, Robert, Watson's view of, 85-86; Watson's elegy on, 115; "Epistle to J. Lapraik," 84

Byron, Lord, mentioned, 72, 92

Caine, Hall, on Watson's early career, 28; compares Watson with Keats, 29; mentioned, 40

Campbell-Bannerman, Sir Henry (prime minister), Watson in sym-

Index

Selected Poems, 162; "Shelley as Poet," 93-94; "Shelley's Centenary," 92-93; "Some Literary Idolatries," 62-63; "Sonnets to Miranda," 151; "The Soudanese," 52; "The Sovereign Poet," 23, 104; "The State Discouragement of Literature," 145-47, 153; "A Sunset," 41; *The Superhuman Antagonists,* 160-61; "Tavern Song," 151; "The Things That Are More Excellent," 87; "The Three Alfreds," 159; "Three Eternities," 44; "Thy voice from inmost dreamland calls," 133; "Time and Tide," 32-33; "To a Friend," 103; "To Arthur Christopher Benson," 103; "To a Strenuous Critic," 158; "To Aubrey De Vere," 102, 124-25; "To Edward Clodd," 77; "To Edward Dowden," 26, 30, 45, 75; "To H. D. Traill," 103; "To One Who Had Written in Derision of the Belief in Immortality," 102, 124; "To the Memory of the Late Sir Henry Campbell-Bannerman," 148-49; "To the Sultan," 122; "A Trial of Orthodoxy," 135; "The Turk in Armenia," 115, 119; "The Two Dorothys," 100; "The Unknown God," 124, 129-30, 134-35; "The Unreconciled," 160-61; "Vanishings," 41; "Ver Tenebrosum," 47-52, 70, 80, 117; "Vita

Nuova," 99, 105; "Wasted Blandishments," 161; "The Woman with the Serpent's Tongue," 148-51; "A Wondrous Likeness," 120; *Wordsworth's Grave and Other Poems,* 19, 77-78, 80-82; "Wordsworth's Grave," 22, 70-74, 76-78, 84, 86, 101, 130, 158; "The World in Armour," 101, 118; "World-Strangeness," 80; "The Yapping Cur," 158; *The Year of Shame,* 118, 123, 141

Watts, G. F. (artist), 119; "The Recording Angel," 122

Webster, John (dramatist), mentioned, 62

Whitman, Walt, Watson critical of, 61; mentioned, 55, 68

Wilde, Oscar, arrest of, 110; Watson's disapproval of, 111; mentioned, 16, 18, 24-25, 59, 83, 101

Wordsworth, William, Watson's attitude toward, 71-76; mentioned, 18, 84-86, 105-6, 118

Yeats, William Butler, and Rhymers' Club, 19-20; on Victorianism, 20, 22; on Watson's *Epigrams,* 48; on "Ver Tenebrosum," 51; review of *Wordsworth's Grave,* 80-81; mentioned, 18, 86

Yellow Book, and Watson, 108, 110-112; decadent flavor of, 16; version of "The Lost Eden" appears in, 130-31; "Hymn to the Sea" appears in, 108